McGILL'S WAR

McGILL'S WAR

A History of Life in Britain During The Great War illustrated by the art of Donald Fraser McGill

John Paul Wilton

FireStep
Press

FireStep Press
An imprint of Firestep Publishing

Gemini House
136–140 Old Shoreham Road
Brighton
BN3 7BD

www.firesteppublishing.com

First published in Great Britain by
Reveille Press 2014

ISBN 978-1-908487-98-8

Cover design by Ryan Gearing

Typeset by Vivian @ Bookscribe

Printed and bound in Great Britain

DEDICATION

This book is dedicated to the current 'Blue Boys', members of
HM Armed Forces who have returned from Theatres of Operation,
including Iraq and Afghanistan.

A donation from the proceeds of the sale of this book will be given
by the author to Canine Partners, who provide assistance dogs for those
with disabilities, including those confined to wheelchairs.

ACKNOWLEDGEMENTS

The estate of Captain Bruce Bairnsfather, for permission to use plates 68, 69, 70 and 136 reproduced by kind permission of Barbara Bruce Littlejohn. James Bissell-Thomas, Donald McGill Museum & Archive, Ryde, Isle of Wight. Brian Lund, Collector and Editor, Picture Post Card Monthly. Andrew Brooks, Collector, for information on Field Service Post Cards and Censor stamps. Kevin Gordon, Curator, Seaford Museum, for research into the life of Lance-Corporal Morden Laws. Michael Partridge, Archivist, Eastbourne College, and Peter Duckers, the Shropshire Museum, for research into the life of Russell Llewellyn Mandeville Lloyd. Diane Ward, for research into the life of Philip Guille of Sark. Ryan Gearing, Publisher, for sourcing additional cards and for much helpful advice. Simon Evers, for transcription of the manuscript. Helen Wilton, for proof-reading the manuscript. Lastly, but by no means least, my wife Elizabeth, for her forbearance over many months.

CONTENTS

Ex-Royal Marine Jon Flint with his canine partner Varick. Photo: Canine Partners.

CANINE PARTNERS

CANINE PARTNERS

Canine Partners is a registered charity that assists people with disabilities to enjoy a greater independence and quality of life through the provision of specially trained dogs, whose well-being is a key consideration.

More than 1.2 million people in the UK use a wheelchair, and a significant number of those would benefit from a canine partner. The dogs are carefully matched to the applicant's needs and lifestyle, no matter how challenging. They are trained to help with everyday tasks such as opening and shutting doors, unloading the washing machine, picking up dropped items, pressing buttons and switches and getting help in an emergency. The Charity aims to train dogs to meet the needs of people with even the most complex disabilities including members of HM Armed Forces, and is working closely with the Forces charity Help for Heroes.

These life transforming dogs also provide practical, physiological, psychological and social benefits including increased independence and confidence as well as increased motivation and self-esteem. A canine partner also brings companionship, a sense of security and increases social interaction.

Canine Partners receives no government funding and relies solely on public donations. For further information visit www.caninepartners.org.uk or phone 08456 580480.

PREFACE

I was inspired to write "McGill's War" after reading "All Quiet on the Home Front, An Oral History of Life in Britain during the First World War" by Richard van Emden and Steve Humphries (2003). The authors used interviews with a very large number of elderly people who lived through the war to create a record of what life was like on the home front during those dark days. As a keen collector of the postcards of Donald McGill, I noticed that his work between 1914 and 1919 mirrored the sentiments expressed by those who had been interviewed. While the authors had the advantage of speaking to those with vivid memories of the time, many years had passed and memories fade, while McGill's postcards (drawn at the time) express the sentiment of the moment and the messages on the cards were also fresh in the minds of those who wrote them. However, it should be noted that the dreaded censor precluded much information being sent home. Some of the words and phrases used have been intentionally left as they were in the original.

INTRODUCTION

It is now too late to listen to the stories of those who lived through the First World War but there are opportunities to read their messages sent on the postcards drawn by Donald McGill. They are not from politicians or generals but from ordinary men and women and their children who were caught up in a conflict that changed their lives and the lives of so many worldwide.

Donald Fraser McGill (28 January 1875 – 13 October 1962)

The name Donald McGill often fails to evoke a response until "saucy seaside postcards" are mentioned. Then memories of racks of cards, positioned outside novelty shops found in holiday resorts such as Blackpool, Brighton,

Hastings and Southend are rekindled. This was back in the 1950's when some of the cards were rightly described as 'saucy'. Many were 'disapproved' by individuals or the local authority and removed from circulation by the police.

However most of McGill's work, which spanned nearly sixty years, from 1904 to 1962, was not saucy and did not feature seaside fun. His early cards featured sporting and business themes but it was his First World War cards, drawn between 1914 and 1919, that show the artist at his best. Few of the cards depict scenes at the Front – McGill concentrated on life at home, including recruits in training, wounded soldiers in convalescent camps, conscientious objectors, rationing and air raids. *McGill's War* uses his cards to capture the mood during the war years and to deliver the message sent to and from France and from towns and villages throughout the United Kingdom. There are even some greetings sent from what was then 'the Colonies'.

The vast majority of McGill's cards used in this book are those published by the Inter-Art Company, Red Lion Square, London WC, which was run by Robert McCrumb. McGill's previous publisher, Joseph Asher, who was a German Jew, was interned on the Isle of Man in 1914, leaving the way open for McCrumb to take over. However, cards published by Asher between 1910 and 1914 were used not only before war was declared but also throughout the war years and even after the cessation of hostilities. Plates 1 to 7 show cards published by Asher.

1. THE EARLY YEARS (1904–1914)

Donald Fraser Gould McGill (1875–1962) started to draw sketches that were turned into postcards in 1904 and the earliest evidence of a McGill postcard is one posted on 29 April in that year. These first designs featured sporting and working themes [1]. Those drawn in 1905 and 1906 are both signed and dated below the drawing.

From 1904 to 1908, McGill worked firstly part-time and then full-time as a freelance artist. From 1908 to 1910, he worked as a 'partner' with Hutson Bros, commonly referred to as Hudson Bros.

The McGill 'partnership' with the Hutson Bros lasted just two years and was only in the nature of an exclusive right to the designs and McGill is reported to have said that he found the relationship between himself and the brothers uncomfortable. 'Womanising and drinking' were words he used when referring to their activities. [2]

Few of the early cards depicted soldiers and those that did showed them in red uniform tunics with blue trousers which had a red stripe down the outside of the leg. It was often implied that the soldiers had an eye for the ladies.

A young lady who is sitting on a bench in the park with her soldier boyfriend says, *"What are you thinking about, Tommy?" "Same as you!"* comes the reply. *"Oh! You naughty man!"* she replies. (E.S. London, no 113, sent on 26 May 1908.) A similar card sent from Cape Town, South Africa in 1907 shows another soldier courting a nursemaid. (E.S. London, no 2083, sent on 10 July 1907.)

A card, unfortunately no postmark visible, was sent by Private F Spencer to his friend Hugh Roycroft: *"Dear Hugh, Just a line to let you no I have listed at last its alright plenty of girls about. When are you coming. I think this is all this time rite back."* Pte F Spencer no 7794 B Company, Chester Castle (E.S. London no 2086.)

In 1910, McGill started working for a new publisher, Joseph Asher, to whom he was contracted to draw a number of sketches each week. This partnership might have lasted until Asher's death in 1951 were it not for the fact that, as a German Jew, Asher was interned as an enemy alien in 1914. When Joseph Asher (Ascher) originally came over from Germany at the start of the 20th century, he anglicized his first name and he dropped the 'c' from his surname intermittently, as shown on the backs of early cards which read 'Published by Joseph Asher & Co., 3 and 4, Ivy Lane, London, EC.'

There was a change in style and choice of subject with Asher. Many more cards featured seaside fun and there were also now cards to celebrate Christmas, birthdays, St Valentine's Day, Leap Year and the New Year. Many people were content to send a card, with a halfpenny stamp, simply to convey greetings. However, there were still few cards showing members of the armed forces – with the exception of those lampooning the Scots in their kilts.

"LEAVE GO, LASSIE — DINNA YE SEE HERE'S TH' COLONEL COMIN!"

Four cards showing soldiers in their red army tunics are interesting. A donkey lifts the kilt of a soldier on guard duty. The sender Kit sends love to Olive.

(No A843) – plate 1

15

(No 1328) – plate 2

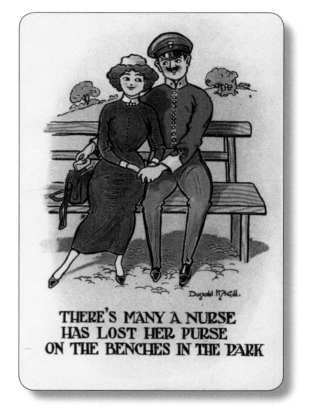

(No A1162) – plate 3

The soldier in a regiment of the line is seen to have wandering hands as does the one sitting with a nurse on a park bench. Doris writes to Edie, *"Just a few lines to let you know I am enjoying myself very much. How do you like this p.c. does it remind you of Richmond Park"*. However, F A Cowdery, Esq receives a Valentine card that most likely did not make his day. It is possible that this card (No A466) – plate 4 – was sent on 13 February 1913 by a suffragette.

(No A466) – plate 4

You funny little rut
How you do strut.
You think the girls
All love you.
We've sent you this
To let you know
We think <u>ourselves</u>
Above you.
Bow Wow.

(No 1343) – plate 5

There was also a series of cards entitled "THE MANOEUVRES" which featured members of the Territorial Army in training. "A NIGHT ATTACK" (No 1343) – plate 5 – was sent from Lowestoft on 13 July 1914 and informs J Johnaw Esq of Meadow Farm, Near Pickenham, Swaffham, Norfolk "I wish I was back at camp". George sends a 'secret' message to Miss Rowena Kelly in Dublin on 9 April 1914 THE LAST POST (No 1341) – plate 6 – *"In case you forget your Georgie while he's away, here's his photo to play with. It was taken at 1am this morning. NEVER MIND."*

(No 1341) – plate 6

ALAS MY POOR BROTHER!! A card (No 1342) – plate 7 – sent by Ruth to Miss E Sergent, c/o A Sergent, Grocer, Forest Gate on 17 April 1914, just over three months before the outbreak of war, implies that the horse meat scandal of 2013 may well not have been the first time that horse meat was substituted for beef.

(No 1342) – plate 7

Other groups in training were the cadets in British public schools. Training for many officers who served in the First World War commenced in their public schools, with weekly parades and a summer camp. Cards sent from an Eastbourne College OTC camp included one (Plate 8) sent on 3 August 1913 from Mytchett by Russell Lloyd to Mrs Joseph Lloyd, Bryndedwydd, St Asaph, North Wales. "*Dear Mother, Thanks awfully for letter. Georgie made us send our luggage home by goods-train to be paid for when it arrived home. If Georgie did not change his mind and send it some other way it should arrive home about last Thursday or Friday. Love to all Rus.*" Russell Lloyd must have left for the summer camp from his boarding school in Eastbourne. 'Georgie' may have been the nickname for his housemaster.

Another card sent home from Eastbourne College on 20 July 1914, just two weeks before the outbreak of hostilities, featured 'B' Company of the school's OTC. Lloyd by then was a Sergeant in the Corps. Research shows that Russell Llewellyn Mandeville Lloyd was born on 21 April 1886 and served in the King's Shropshire Light Infantry from 1914 to 1918. He finished the war as a

Captain, was wounded twice, mentioned in dispatches and awarded an MC and Bar and the Croix de Guerre avec etoile. Between the wars he worked as a solicitor, practising in Rhyl, North Wales. Lloyd returned to the KSLI during the 2nd Word War. His death is recorded on 19 January 1959.

(Plate 8)

Although Joseph Asher was interned on the Isle of Man in 1914, his cards continued to be postally used throughout and even after the war years. Some have messages to or from the troops at the front or reveal interesting events at home.

Here's a fine view of an internment camp! (also in French) 'Comique' series (No 2433) – plate 9 – sent from Dudley on 10 August 1920 to the Drawing Office, Humber Ltd, Humber Road, Coventry. "*Dear Lis, Just a line to let you know we are having a posh time, writing this by Dudley Castle, plenty of boys, so you may guess we are A1. Been to several places didn't know were on the map, Yours etc B.E.F.*" The card produced and postally used some

Here's a fine view of an internment camp!
Un camp de concentration.

(No 2433) – plate 9

years after the outbreak of hostilities shows a rotund gentleman who seems to have fared very well while interned. Could this be a dig at Joseph Asher after confinement?

On 4 August 1914, the day Britain declared war on Germany, Alex wrote to Mr H North in Blackpool, *"Dear Harry, How now! I've been on duty except Monday. Will you have to show a leg? Cheer up and have just a wee one with me. Yours, Alex."* (No A432).

Miss Annie Mitchell of Bristol received a card sent on 23 October 1914, *"Leaving here tomorrow Saturday don't no where to. Good luck have a stout Old Dear."* (No A442).

Jim, on active service, sent a card on 5 June 1916 via Army P.O. 3 and the Field Censor to Miss Evans in London, *"I am alright hope you are well, fine week but colder today with rain. Fairly busy. Has your brother come out here yet. Yours sincerely Jim."* (No A942).

2. WAR DECLARED

War had been triggered on 28 June when Archduke Franz Ferdinand, heir to the Austro-Hungarian throne, was assassinated in Sarajevo by Gavrilo Princip, a Bosnian-Serbian student. Austria, which was allied with Germany in the Triple Alliance and was anxious to increase its control of the Balkans, issued an ultimatum to Serbia, demanding a part in the investigation into the shooting and the suppression of anti-Austrian movements within Serbia. The inevitable Serb refusal was followed by an Austrian declaration of war against Serbia.

Russia, Serbia's ally, ordered a general mobilization. Germany in turn responded and on August 1 declared war on Russia. Berlin saw the sudden crisis as a golden opportunity to destroy not just Russia but Russia's allies in the Triple Entente – France and Britain. On August 3, the Germans declared war on France and the following day invaded Belgium. Britain promptly declared war against Germany and Austria declared war against Russia. The First World War had begun.[3]

No-one wanted to contemplate a war lasting beyond Christmas time, just five months away. There was an inherent public belief in the capabilities of the British army when called to action. However, most military commanders, Lord Kitchener among them, saw that the war would be anything but short. Britain's small, highly trained regular army was no match in terms of numbers for the huge German forces which, within a week of mobilisation, had 3.8 million men under arms. Kitchener foresaw that a new citizens' army would be required, made up of volunteers.

The British government had envisaged that, in terms of war, the regular and territorial armies would simply grow organically, taking on recruits and expanding as required. Lord Kitchener, who had little enough faith in the prowess of the new Territorial Force, decided to discard the idea and, as the new Secretary of State for War, create an entirely new army of 100,000 men. However, such was the apparent enthusiasm to fight that three times that number of civilians enlisted in August before word even got out that this new army was needed. Then, when Kitchener launched his famous appeal, epitomised by the poster 'Your Country Needs You', there came a second, spontaneous response with hundreds of thousands of men besieging recruiting stations set up right across the country.[4]

So many volunteers flocked to the colours – a million in the first three months – that they had to wear civilian clothes and use dummy weapons for training. They spent much time on bayonet drill. However, bayonets accounted for a mere one percent of war casualties.[5]

THEY USED TO CALL US 'TERRIERS' BUT NOW WE ARE 'BOYS OF THE BULL-DOG BREED'! 'PATRIOTIC' series VII, (No 864) – plate 10 – British production. Inter-Art Co., Red Lion Square, London WC. (Not postally used.) A soldier in the Territorial army is holding a newspaper, presumably dated August 5 1914, which declares the outbreak of war. Many cards in the 'Patriotic' series have a red, white and blue border.

(No 864) – plate 10

'Comique' series (No 1543) – plate 11.

"**Don't worry, I'll soon be back**". Not dated or stamped. Private Thomas (Tommy Atkins) is on his way to Berlin – his army number no 1234567 is incorrect, as army numbers in 1914–15 were just four or five digits. J C Jones writes, "*Dear Father landed O.K. Remember me to all – Hope are allright as I am. Love Your Loving son J C Jones.*"

'Comique' series (No 1461) – plate 12.

Not signed or dated:
"*The War'll be over in a fortnight now, 'cos my ole man's joined the Army an' I know 'e never keeps a job longer 'n that!*" The writer has added, "*Now Auntie Don't take this too seriously.*"

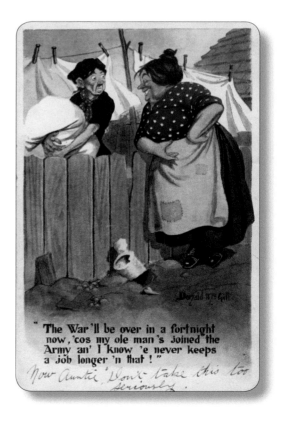

(No 811) – plate 13.

HATS OFF!! (to Belgium) 'PATRIOTIC' series IV (No 811) – plate 13 – sent on 6 November 1914 was used to send Birthday good wishes to Mr R H Shaw Junior of Shipston on Stour.

(No 959) – plate 14.

UNDER TWO FLAGS, 'R.C.' series (No 959) – plate 14 – shows Britain and France united. The card was sent from Grahamstown, South Africa to Rosebank, Cape Province. McGill's cards were available in many Commonwealth countries.

WELL, HE LOOKS A BIT BIG, BUT HE'LL JUST ABOUT MAKE A MEAL FOR THE THREE OF US! PATRIOTIC series IV (No 813) – plate 15 – sent from West Brompton, SW (London) on 24 October 1914 to Master L W Lamport, 3 Witham Rod, Anerley, Surrey. "*With love to Lennie & lots of kisses on his birthday from Cousin Kenneth Auntie Edith sends love to you and Cissy.*" The French poodle, Russian bear and English bulldog hope to make a 'meal' of a German sausage.

(No 813) – plate 15.

(No 818) – plate 16 – front and reverse.

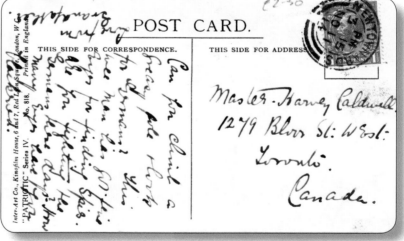

HAS ANYONE SEEN A GERMAN BAND? 'PATRIOTIC' series IV (No 818) – plate 16 – sent on 11 November 1914 from Newtownards in Northern Ireland to Master Harvey Caldwell, Toronto, Canada. Harvey's grandfather writes, "*Can you climb a greasy pole and look for Germans? This wee man has got fine eyes for finding spies. Are you fighting the Germans these days? How many eyes have you blackened? Love from Grandfather.*"

Early cards postally used during the war include those in the 'ARMEE' series. On number 910 – plate 17 – *BEFORE YOU FOOL WITH A FOOL BE SURE YOU'VE A FOOL TO FOOL WITH!* Ada writes, "*Dear Dad. I hope you are quite well. Tommy is out playing English and Germans. If you had been at Southport I would have come over at whit week even if I had to pay for myself. Hope you arrive safe at the South of England. With love from Ada.*" The card is not dated but may well have been sent in June or July 1915.

(No 910) – plate 17.

(No 912) – plate 18.

Card number 912 – plate 18 – in the same series, *IT'S A LONG, LONG WAY TO – - - PARIS!* (Also in French) "La Route de Paris" – not a translation and one that fails to express the sentiment that the Germans will find it a long and punishing journey. Jack, on active service, sends the card on 28 October 1915 from Army PO 3 via the censor to his wife Mrs Mabel Mackness of Plaistow, London. "*My Dear Mabel – Thanks for letter rec' today, glad you are quite well, the weather here is very bad just at present, hope you rec' my letter sent yesterday & card very best love Jack.*" The card, which is written in pencil, is signed by Leslie Clarkson, who may well have been a junior officer who was required to censor his men's letters.

I THINK YOU CALLED? A third card in the 'Armee' series (No 908) – plate 19 – was posted on 23 March 1915 and sent to Miss Burden c/o Mrs Cooper of Upper Edmington. *"Dear Vera will you let us no how Uncle Cooper his love to all from son XXXXX"* During the early years of the war, large numbers of Indian soldiers enlisted to help the mother country in her hour of need.

(No 908) – plate 19

3. RECRUITS

The 'RECRUITS' series, widely used in 1915, featured those who had volunteered to serve in Lord Kitchener's New Army. In many cases, it took a full year for the new civilian soldiers to be fully trained and, although some volunteers left for France in 1915, most Kitchener men would not see action until the following year.

I SHAN'T COME BACK WITH A SCAR ANYWAY! (No 920) – plate 20 – was posted on 19 August 1915 by Jack to his mother, Mrs Dickinson.

(No 920) – plate 20.

I'M NOT HALF PICKING UP SINCE I JOINED THE ARMY! (No 921) – plate 21. Lillie writes on 25 February 1915 to her father Mr Todd in Dover *"Dr Father Thought you would like this P.C. How did you like your cigarettes, did you get them alright, cannot say more now, with heaps of love Lillie."*

(No 910) – plate 21.

(No 922) – plate 22.   (No 925) – plate 23.   (No 266) – plate 24.

WELL, I'VE DONE MY BIT IF I NEVER SEE A GERMAN! (No 922) – plate 22.
On this card, also posted in 1915, George writes to his father Mr R Brewer in
Deoonport (sic) *"Dear D Just a line to say that I got your P.C. alright I am
in the best of Health so I hope you are look after tiny for me so I must close
now from George."* [Was tiny George's dog?]

"KITCHENER'S?" – NOT HALF!! (No 925) – plate 23 – Cocoa is being prepared
for Kitchener's Recruits, sent on April 22 1916 by Cousin Hilda to Master Fred
Le Riche, St Helier, Jersey, C.I. *"Dear Fred, Thanks so much for reminder and
for the key of the bungo. I'm glad to see it is still there and wish I lived as
near to it as you do. Hoping to see it and you all if I don't get torpedoed.
With love from Cousin Hilda."* Was the bungo a secret camp? Interesting
reference to the threat from German U boats.

KITCHENER WANTS 1,000,000 – but I'd be satisfied with far less, so come and
join me. TWO-SIX-THREE Series (No 266) – plate 24 – sent from Birmingham
on 25 August 1915 to Miss Murray, Arnside, Westmoreland. *"Mind the
Postman gives you this alright. I passes no remarks on it, as it is from your
beloved 'Birmingham'."*

1000000 MORE MEN WANTED – THE STORK:- "SAY, I'D BETTER GET BUSY!!"
ONE-SIX-ONE Series (No 169) – plate 25 – Liz sent this card to her mother on
24 December 1915: *"Dear Mother as I could not get you a goose for Xmas I
have got something very near hope you will enjoy the turkey from Liz."*

(No 169) – plate 25.

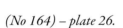

(No 164) – plate 26.

KITCHENER WANTS MORE MEN! WHAT I'M DOING FOR MY COUNTRY !
Series ONE-SIX-ONE (No 164) – plate 26 – (also in French) – not postally
used. Many cards have captions in both English and French, indicating that
they were also intended for sale in France and Belgium.[6]

The three cards proclaim the fact that Lord Kitchener wanted to create a New Army of 1,000,000 men – a long term project perhaps!

Monday 3 August 1914 was a Bank Holiday and recruiting offices were closed but for the rest of the week. There was an average of 1,600 volunteers a day signing on: between 4 August and 12 September, 478,893 men enlisted.[7]

There were many reasons for volunteering. These included patriotism, the desire for adventure and the belief that the army offered an escape from unemployment or a humdrum existence. Young men enlisted as groups of friends. There was also an element of pressure from newspapers, the Church, displays on hoardings – and McGill's postcards.

Life in the army came as a shock for many of the volunteers. First there was the medical inspection and once passed fit for training, Reveille, at a time many recruits considered to be the middle of the night and then during their training a lecture by the M.O.!

They hopped me here
They hopped me there
Until I felt quite barmy
They felt my pulse an' told me to "Cough!"
And passed me into the Army.

'Comique' series (No 1786) – plate 27 – not postally used.

"Christians awake!" 'Comique' series (No 1777) – plate 28 – sent on 8 March 1917 to C/12144 Gn. J G Smith, Royal Marine Artillery, Heavy Liege Train, BF c/o GPO London. *"So glad you are well and comfortable. I have written <u>twice</u> to this same address. Have you had them yet. We are having some mild weather again,*

(No 1786) – plate 27.

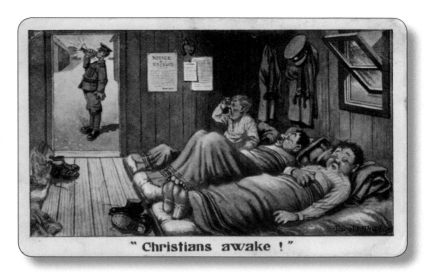

(No 1777) – plate 28.

plenty of rain, etc. We are still very busy spring cleaning, Edi helping us.
Theo is going to Eastbourne soon. I think he wants Mum to go to. It will do
her good won't it. Hope you are well.
Yours Kit."

A Lecture on Love (by the Medical
Officer). 'Comique' series (No 1783) –
plate 29 – not postally used.

McGill suggested that, especially during
basic training, the recruits had little free
time.

RECRUITS ORDERS OF THE DAY
8 HOURS DRILL
8 ″ (ROUTE MARCH)
8 ″ TRENCHING –
AND THEN WE HAVE THE REST OF
THE DAY TO OURSELVES!

(No 1783) – plate 29.

'RECRUITS' series (No 923) – plate 30 – sent from Marlborough Lines on 23 February 1915 to Miss P Kneeshaw, North Gate, Market Weighton, E Yorks. *"Dear P, I thought you would just ? to let you know that we have started off today. So I will let you know when we arrive. Happy as a King. Hoping you are the same from yours – - – -"* It could well be that the writer was off to France in the next draft.

"Please, can you tell me the way to the 'Soldiers' Rest"?
"'Soldier's Rest'! Bless yer, mate – they don't get any!!!"

(No 923) – plate 30.

"Please, can you tell me the way to
the 'Soldiers' Rest'?"
"'Soldiers' Rest'! Bless yer, mate—
they don't get any!!!"

(No 2286) – plate 31.

'Comique' series (No 2286) – Plate 31 – not postally used. Apart from drill, route marches with heavy packs, there was work to be done in the field kitchens, heaving coal for fires and generally keeping the camp clean and tidy up to the standard demanded by senior N.C.O.s – and when that was done there had to be time for bulling boots and mending kit.

"FULL MARCHING ORDER"
WHAT YOUR KIT FEELS LIKE
AFTER TEN MILES !

(No 174) – plate 32.

"DADDY, WHAT DID YOU DO
IN THE GREAT WAR ?"

(No 1331) – plate 33.

I wonder if there is anyone else in the Army
doing anything besides me!

(No 2054) – plate 34.

"FULL MARCHING ORDER"
WHAT YOUR KIT FEELS LIKE AFTER TEN MILES!
'K.A.' series – (No 174) – plate 32 — not postally used.

Field Kitchen no 6 *"DADDY, WHAT DID YOU DO IN THE GREAT WAR?"*
'Comique' series (No 1331) – plate 33 – not postally used.

I wonder if there is anyone else in the Army doing anything besides me! –
'Comique' series (No 2054) – plate 34 – sent on 15 July 1918.

Say, Bill, how did Noah manage to get two of these blighters into the Ark?
(Also in French) – 'Comique' series (No 2184) – plate 35 – sent on 5 February
1918 to Pte Fred Bacon, 3rd Bat Royal Sussex Reg. *"Dear Fred, Just a PC in
answer to yours just received. I don't know a chap like that. Give my love to
Grace and Winnie. I am going on allright. Le is at Chatham. Hope you are
A1 as it leaves us all. Don't work to hard. Hope to hear from you soon. With
love   XXXXXX"*

(No 2184) – plate 35.

I'm only just sew-sew at present. (Also in French.) 'Comique' series (No 1987) – plate 36 – postmark illegible as stamp removed. Signed "Pauline van Damme" and sent to an address in Bruxelles (Brussels).

(No 1987) – plate 36 – front and reverse.

4. BLUE BOYS

From the earliest days of the war, wounded soldiers arrived back in Britain bound for military hospitals and then military convalescent camps. One such camp was situated from 1915 to 1920 in Eastbourne, East Sussex, in the area now occupied by Compton Drive, Old Camp Road and Pashley Road. In 1915 this camp housed up to 3,500 troops. These soldiers were required to wear not their khaki uniform but blue trousers and tunics with a white shirt and red tie. They were therefore known as the Blue Boys. If the trousers were too long, they were turned up, as faithfully drawn by McGill.

An early card showing the camp and dated 10 September 1915 was sent to Mrs A Lansdell, Clapham Road, Stockwell, London SW. "Glad to hear news from Herbert. Am very comfortable & having fine weather. Love to all Dad."

Albert 'Smiler Marshall quoted in *Last Post* said, "*I was wounded at Mametz Wood and I landed up in Rouen Hospital, with a bullet through my hand amongst other wounds. The boat bringing the wounded back docked at Newcastle, and I was sent to convalesce in Eastbourne. They dressed me in blue with a white shirt and red tie so that everyone could see that I had been wounded. When I had recovered, they sent me to Aldershot to re-train . . .*" [8]

SUMMERDOWN CAMP B LINES – plate 37 – sent on October 9 1915

BLUE BOYS IN THEIR HUT SUMMERDOWN CAMP – plate 38 – sent on 21 October 1915.

Both photos: CROMPTONS, Photographers, 32/34 High Street, Old Town, Eastbourne.[9]

'POOR MAN! AND HAVE YOU BEEN WOUNDED AT THE FRONT'
'NO, MA'AM – AT THE BACK!'

TWELVE-THIRTY-EIGHT Series (No 1243) – plate 39 – sent on 3 May 1917 to Miss Marsh in Oxford.

(No 1243) – plate 39 – sent 3 May 1917

HE LOOKED SMARTER IN KHAKI – BUT I LOVE HIM BEST IN THIS! THE FRONT Series (No 1217) – plate 40 – sent from Chard, shows an accurate portrait of the uniform and implies that the wounded soldiers will be both loved and admired.

"In hospitals and convalescent homes, flirtations, fantasies, romance and intimate bonding captivated both patients and staff, especially at Christmas time. Indeed many women met their future husbands in the wards."[10]

(No 1217) – plate 40

(No 1124) – plate 41

"BADLY HIT – CONDITION SERIOUS!" ELEVEN-TWENTY-TWO Series (No 1124) – plate 41 – sent from Margate on 28 July 1916 to Mr Thomas of Islington. McGill illustrated this intimate bonding. The nurse and the patient are not only holding hands but would seem to be sharing a bed. Are they breaking hospital rules?

All I need is sympathy! 'Comique' series (No 2049) – plate 42 – dated and sent 10 November 1917 from Shorncliffe (Kent) to Miss V Muggeridge, Jubilee Hospital, Woodford Green, Essex. "*Dear Vi, Am going back to May next week, will drop you a line on the boat, as I'm too busy now. Sorry I cannot come to see you before I go, but we shall meet again, if not here, then up above. Best love and wishes Bert XXXX*". There are several unanswered questions: Was Bert going back to France? Was Vi a nurse? Had Bert been a Blue Boy? Who was May?

(No 2049) – plate 42

(No 2186) – plate 43

All seats on public transport were made available to the Blue Boys for free, as was entry to zoos, cinemas and most theatres. Many of the soldiers received gifts of packets of cigarettes or chocolate.

Woodbine cigarettes were available in paper packets of 5. Card 'Comique' series (No 2186) – plate 43 – says it all: "*And what are your favourite flowers? WILD WOODBINES, Mum!*"

'Comique' series card (No 2545) – plate 44 – "*Regret we have been compelled to retire!*" (TO DOCK – added by Billy). On 19 November 1918 (shortly after the end of hostilities) Billy writes to Miss Phyl Mitchell of Willesden, London, "*Dear Phyl, Just a few lines to say that I am in blues. (Hospital.) Will be out tomorrow so will give you all the news later Love XX Billy XX.*" The postmark, only partly legible, Ly---- Kent (may have been Lyminge).

(No 2545) – plate 44

On a card showing Summerdown Camp and sent from Eastbourne on 24 March 1918 to Miss E Harvey of St Luke's, Jersey, Jack writes, "*My Darling Just arrived at this place & it is fine. We are quite close to the beach & as the weather is glorious it is top hole. I am getting on fine but my arm is still painful. However bless just look what I am missing. The Germans have started their great push just where I was. I hope to be home soon & it will be lovely as weather is coming on. Write soon Dear yours for Ever Jack. This is the photo of our camp. D Div 17 Hut Summerdown Convalescent Camp, Eastbourne.*"

The 'great push' was the Ludendorff Offensive which began on 21 March 1918. The General targeted the lightly held British front on the old Somme battlefield, perhaps the weakest point in the line. The casualty list of men killed or wounded was immense, the Germans losing 348,000, the French 112,000 and the British 343,000.

Another card showing the Summerdown Camp was posted by Pte G W Cooper 103842 to Miss E Day. Ivy Cottage, Ickleford, Near Hitchen, Herts on 15 July 1917 from Blackpool. Private Cooper gives his address as 4 Hut, 4 Line, B section, Ripon Training Camp, No 3 Camp, Blackpool, Lancs. *"Dearest E, Have arrived here safe and sound at 9pm after a fine journey. I saw your Dad and mine at Euston. We are in tents 7 in one tent all different boys. Cheer up, dear – God bless you with love George."* George may well have been transferred from the Eastbourne camp to the one in Blackpool. (*See Loos Trenches* p.90).

5. CONSCIENTIOUS OBJECTORS

Only 16,100 men and women took advantage of a clause in the Military Service Act to register as conscientious objectors. Among them were Bertrand Russell, Fenner Brockway and Sylvia Pankhurst, the suffragette. The overwhelming strength of public opinion was behind the war and it took immense courage to become a 'conchie'. Many were subjected to abuse and violence. Pacifist meetings were often broken up by mobs, sometimes with the collusion of the police.

At the local tribunals that determined their fate, 80% of conscientious objectors were granted some form of exemption from military service. 3,300 joined the non-Combatant Corps, 2,400 worked in ambulances or as stretcher-bearers at the front, 3,964 took up work on the home front, many working on road building schemes and 6,261 men were sent to prison.

It was the absolutists who refused to do war work of any sort who suffered most. Some were forcibly sent to the front. If they continued to refuse to obey orders, they could in theory be shot. In all, 71 pacifists died in prison as a result of injuries sustained there. They became martyrs to the cause but, to the majority of the population, they were just 'shirkers', 'cowards' and 'traitors'.[11]

McGill's cards mirror the anger and contempt felt by many towards conscientious objectors, especially for those who tried to avoid the front by appearing before a local tribunal. However, the messages sent, with one exception, do not match the sentiment expressed by the illustrator:

Thank the Lord I aint got a conscience (Also in French). 'ARTISTIQUE' series (No 1431) – plate 45 – sent on 20 February 1917. Field Post Office – Passed by Censor. Eddie, on active service and part of the B.E.F., writes to Miss Wilcock of Dewsbury, Yorkshire *"My dear Nell, Going on A1. My cold is very much better. Hope you are quite well again. Writing letter tomorrow. Kindest regards to all Best love Eddie."*

(No 1431) – plate 45

(No 1428) – plate 46

Who's the old Tribunal anyway – I haven't exempted you!! 'ARTISTIQUE'
series (No 1428) – plate 46 – sent on 9 August 1917. From Portsmouth, Auntie
Minnie writes to Master Harold Chapman of Tring, Herts. *"Dr Harold I have
not forgotten your Birthday but my little present will be late, sorry, but
better late than never, hope you will have a happy Birthday & many of them
With love from Auntie Minnie XXXX."*

But, dammit man, I dont want to be exempted!! 'Comique' series (No 1474)
– plate 47 – sent on 5 October 1917 From Blackpool to Mr & Miss Ryder of
Shipley, Yorkshire, M.S. writes, *"Dear Mrs – staying at Blackpool for a little
while. Arthur here too. Having a good time. Grand weather. Best love to
both M.S."*

IN THE DARDAN-OH! 'ELL – ES!! (Also in French) TWO-O-THREE series
(No 205) – plate 48 – sent from Pau, France (just north of the Pyrenees) to
Mademoiselle Bernoiselle, St Jean de ? The date has been erased. The one
word 'conche' for correspondence and the drawing of the shell about to
penetrate the ample posterior of the Turkish man who is not in uniform
could be construed as a threat to the well-being of Mademoiselle and / or
her family.

(No 1474) – plate 47   *(No 205) – plate 48*

6. SPECIAL CONSTABLES

The police force was depleted as many officers had been called up for duty at the front. In their place, thousands of special constables were recruited – 20,000 in London alone. They were predominantly elderly men and no match for a fleet-footed young thief. One of their tasks was to enforce the blackout when Zeppelin raids were predicted. The special constables also guarded potential targets such as the local gas works. McGill's first series shows the Special Constables guarding important locations including a reservoir.

NO OLE GERMAN STEALS THIS RESERVOIR! S.C.P. 1st series (No 955) – plate 49 – sent from Brighton on 8 August 1915. In the second series they are attempting to keep law and order in the country.

(No 955) – plate 49

(No 113) – plate 50

NOW, IF YOU DON'T MOVE ON I – I – I SHALL CALL A POLICEMAN!! 'S.P.C.' 2nd series (No 113) – plate 50 — sent on 23 April 1915 from Tottenham to P Turner Esq. Streatham Hill, S.W. *"Dear Uncle, Arthur has just gone home after coming to spend the afternoon with us & I went to the pictures with him. He asked me if it would be convenient if he came + Jo to Streatham on Tuesday night? The special constables are here too. This is you when you patrol the streets your trousers are not like the badger though truly Eric."*

(No 114) – plate 51.   *(No 115) – plate 52.*   *(No 116) – plate 53.*

"LUMMY, GUV'NOR, 'OW YOU FRIGHTENED ME! I THOUGHT AT FUST YOU WAS A COPPER!!" 'S.P.C.' 2nd series (No 114) – plate 51 – sent on 15 November 1917 London W.C. to Miss Agnes, West End Lane, Pinner *"My dear Agnes, Be so kind as to excuse this p.c. on your birthday. I hope it will be a very happy one. I intended getting you something but have not had a minute to spare lately, but you will have it later. Hope you are better I should have gone to the (Hobbn?) if you had come today. Bye Bye for now am just off to work. Much love from Aunt Sally & myself."*

YOU WILL BE CHARGED WITH PLAYIN' SHOVE HA'PENNY WITH FELONIUS INTENT! 'S.P.C.' 2nd series (No 115) – plate 52 – sent on 14 April 1915 Caterham Valley, Surrey, readdressed 16 April 1915 from Gillingham, Kent, to no 4437 Lance Corporal G Wellmer, 3rd Batt Queen's, Queen's Camp, Fortbridgewood, Rochester *"My Dear just a card to you to say we are all quite well hope you are the same Dear I hope you like the card. Dear Daddy I don't like the card the old Devil is making the boys cry to much here love from . . . .? XXXX"*

A BOMB!! 'S.P.C.' 2nd series (No 116) – plate 53 – not postally used.

7. ALLOTMENTS

To ensure that Britain would not be starved into surrender, there had to be an immediate increase in food production at home.[12] In the towns and cities, the nation's gardeners answered the call to increase the supply of food. An army of the elderly, mothers, housewives, munitions workers and their children picked up their forks and spades and worked in allotments. Common land, parks and playing fields were dug up and planted. King George V decreed that potatoes, cabbages and other vegetables should replace geraniums in the flower beds opposite Buckingham Palace. The allotment campaign was a great success. By the end of the war, there would be over 90,000 acres under allotments, almost four times the total when war began.[13]

WHAT DID YOU DO IN THE GREAT WAR, DADDY? 'Comique' series (No 2643) – plate 54 – not postally used.

(No 2643) – plate 54.

8. ALCOHOL

(No 1042) – plate 55

In August 1914, the Government regulated opening hours in pubs, mainly those in the centres of the munitions industry and ports. However, in 1917, the restrictions were extended all over the country. Some pubs only opened for three or four hours a day. Many opened only at lunch time and others that did open in the evening closed as early as 9pm.

In addition, liquor duties, imposed to raise money for the war effort, meant that the price of a pint tripled in three years. At the same time, the Government progressively lowered the permitted alcohol content of beers and spirits.

Assisting the Government in its campaign to stamp out the evils of excessive drinking were the Temperance Movement and the Social Purity Movement, in which the churches played a leading role.[14]

As a contribution to the war effort, in 1915 King George V announced that he and the royal household were to abstain from alcohol for the duration. The King's abstention was intended to set an example, particularly to workers in the shipyards and armaments factories, whose heavy drinking was said to be holding up weapons production.

In October 1915, buying a round of drinks, "treating", was made illegal on pain of a £100 fine (£6,500 today) or six months imprisonment. Also outlawed was the publican's "on the house" offer to a favoured customer.[15]

Although weak beer and early closing were universally derided, they were endured with stoicism and resulted in a reduction in alcohol consumption.[16]

"NOW LET 'EM DO THEIR WORST!!" 'Protection" series (No 1042) – plate 55 – no date or postmark.

9. SEPARATION ALLOWANCES

For those whose husbands had gone to war, there were separation allowances to offset the loss of income. The rate was 12/6 (62p) a week, with an extra 2/- (10p) for each child. The amounts rarely compensated the family for the financial loss, and while soldiers at the front could allocate part of their wages to families at home, any allowance from a private's pay of 7/- (35p) a week was likely to be meagre.[17] Wives whose husbands were killed, but then formed an attachment with another man had their separation allowances stopped because of allegedly 'immoral behaviour'. Those who re-married often fared little better financially and socially, especially if their new husband was not liked by their children.[18]

"Hi Alice! Come an' get yer Separation Allowance!"
'Comique' series (No 1727) – plate 56 – not dated or postmarked. The message is written in French.

(No 1727) – plate 56.

10. LICE

Lice infestation was the norm in the trenches and it is estimated that up to 97 per cent of officers and men who lived in the trenches were afflicted with lice. Men who returned home on leave were not likewise affected and the end of the war in November 1918 brought an end to the problem of infestation. The conditions in the trenches proved ideal for the rapid spread of lice which could only thrive in warm conditions which were provided by body heat and clothing.

To spread from person to person lice required close proximity of a new potential host and this was readily provided as men huddled together to preserve a degree of warmth. Of the three types of lice (head, pubic and body) the latter was far and away the most common.[19]

Albert 'Smiler' Marshall (1897 – 2005) stated:
'I think the worst thing of the whole war was being so lousy – we hated the lice.' [20]

Harry Patch (1898 – 2009), the last of the fighting Tommies, remembered lice well. *'We were lousy. The lice were the size of grains of rice, each with its own bite, each with its own itch. When we could, we would run hot wax from a candle down the seams of our trousers, our vests – whatever you had – to burn the buggers out. It was the only thing to do.'* [21]

I've got a chum in my company who sticks closer to me than a brother! 'Comique' series (No 2131) – plate 57 – not dated or postmarked. Arthur writes to his sister Lilian:
"My dearest Lily, this is to say that I have got here all right and feel d – - n sorry for it too, I

I've got a chum in my company who sticks to me closer than a brother !

(No 2131) – plate 57.

*don't like Seaford it looks better than it did when I was here before but still I
don't like the place . . ."*

We always come up to scratch. 'Comique' series (No 2391) – plate 58 – not
dated.

Say, Bill, that bloke must have been in the trenches!
'Comique' series (No 2052) – plate 59 – not postally used.

We always come up to the scratch.

(No 2391) – plate 58.

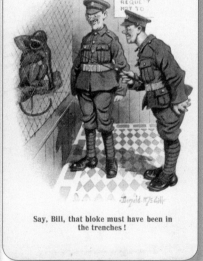

Say, Bill, that bloke must have been in
the trenches !

(No 2052) – plate 59.

"Yes, I went through the whole
War without a scratch!"
"Good Lord! What insect powder
did you use?"

(No 2791) – plate 60.

*"Yes, I went through the whole war without a scratch!" "Good Lord, what
insect powder did you use?"* 'Comique' series (No 2791) – plate 60 – sent on
30 August 1919 from Battersea SW. The card was drawn and posted after the
end of the war. Powders were available to protect the soldiers against bites
but it was said that they were not very effective.

11. YOUR COUNTRY NEEDS YOU

From the start of hostilities, Donald McGill did his bit to help the drive for volunteers to enlist. Conscription for single men was introduced in January 1916 and in April it was extended to married men between 18 and 41. Those who did not enlist of their own volition began to be targeted by all kinds of insidious propaganda. McGill used the trick of putting children in situations which could then be transferred to adults and in particular he used the theme of girls only choosing to give their affections to the soldier and sailor boys. Children, even girls, were shown as being desperate to enlist and do their bit, the implication being that young men should be ready to do this as a matter of course.[22]

I __will__ be a Boy! 'Comique' series (No 1460) – plate 61 – sent from London SW on 7 August 1916.

(No 1460) – plate 61 – front and reverse

I CAN LOOK THE GIRLS IN THE FACE NOW! (also in French) 'Comique' series (No 1395) – plate 62 – dated 12 October 1917, and sent by a father to his son. *"Dear Freddy, I thought you would like a card from Dear Dad. I hope you are enjoying your little self. Wish I could have a game with you. Hope you love XXX dear Mum and Alice love XXXX from your loving Dad."*

(No 1395) – plate 62.

(No 1238) – plate 63.

YOUR SUIT DOESN'T APPEAL TO ME! TWELVE-THIRTY-EIGHT Series (No 1238) – plate 63 – sent from Grantham on 25 April 1916.

By far and away the best known weapon used against 'shirkers' was the white feather, the hard-hitting public sign of cowardice that was vigorously awarded by women to men 'not yet in khaki'. Male civilians were harangued everywhere, with boys as young as 15 or 16 being given feathers, as were married men over 40, neither group being sought for enlistment. Even men who had enlisted were targets, for the dire shortage of uniforms forced many to drill in civilian clothes for weeks before wearing khaki.
In 1915, those who had registered for the Derby Scheme, whereby they asserted to serve but were not called until needed, were issued with khaki armbands with a red crown to prevent mistakes and their embarrassment.[23]

"AS NOW WORN" (Also in French) 'Comique' series (No 1386) – plate 64 – sent on 14 July 1916 from Rotterdam to Den Haag (the Hague) may have been passed by a censor (A373).

(No 1386) – plate 64.

"AS NOW WORN."
"Cela cache mes vaccins."

WHERE'S YOURS? 'Comique' series (No 1332) – plate 65 – sent from Woolwich on 19 July 1916 by Dolly to her uncle Mr. G. Hewitt, Raynes Park, Wimbledon. *"Dear Uncle Just a card hoping you are all well I am staying at Woolwich for a month I don't know if I might come to Wimbledon for a week & see you or not I am staying with a soldier's wife that's been staying with me at Twyford My address is Mrs G Mansell, c/o Mrs Taylor, 678 Woolwich Road, Charlton, London SE. I came here last Friday. Give my love to all Dolly."* Was Mrs Marshall still married? Was her husband alive and serving in the Forces?

(No 1332) – plate 65.

(No 1882) – plate 66 – front and reverse.

Protection had also to be given to those in reserved occupations, including farmers, many of whom remained on their farms to provide food for the nation.

"Why aren't you at the Front, my man?"
"'Cos there aint no milk that end, Miss!!"
'Comique' series (No 1882) – plate 66 – sent by Cousin Cissy from Ashton-under-Lyme on 6 July 1917 to Everybody at 108 Swan Lane, Hindley Green, Near Wigan.

Those who were involved in the manufacture of aircraft were also required to remain at their posts.

"And what work are you doing of National Importance?"
"Why, I'm rearin' eight children an' helping to make airyplanes!"
'Comique' series (No 2331) – plate 67 – not postally used.

"And what work are you doing of National Importance?"
. "Why, I'm rearin' eight children an' helping to make airyplanes!"

(No 2331) – plate 67.

However, it should be noted that many of these cards were sent to young children and women and were not used to persuade the recipient to enlist.

12. AT THE FRONT

Very few cards drawn by McGill depict life at the front. For that we must go to Captain Bruce Bairnsfather and his postcards, 'Fragments from France', which were available from May 1916 in nine packets of six cards. The cards, printed in England, were an instant success but few were sent by soldiers serving overseas.[24] Both artists featured shells bursting and plum and apple jam, both much disliked by the troops. It would seem that the quality and flavour of the jam was important, so much so that the much-maligned plum and apple jam, the kind most frequently supplied to the 'other ranks', was lampooned in "Plum and Apple", rendered to the tune of "A Wee Dioch an' Doris":

Plum and apple
Apple and plum
There is always some.
The A.S.C. gets strawberry jam
And lashings of rum.
But we poor blokes
We only get
Apple and plum.[25]

The Things that Matter, series 1 –
plate 68. © 2013 Barbara Bruce Bairnsfather.
All rights reserved.

In *The Things that Matter,* series 1 – plate 68 – not postally used, Colonel Fitz-Shrapnel is asked by GHQ during a heavy bombardment how many tins of raspberry jam have been issued, and in *The Eternal Question,* series 2 – plate 69 – Old Bill mutters "When the 'ell is it goin' to be strawberry?".

Another Bairnsfeather card, *That Evening Star-Shell* – plate 70 – depicting a soldier flat on his stomach as a star shell bursts above him, was sent from Worcester on 1 January 1917 to Miss J Whitbread, Wesley House, London

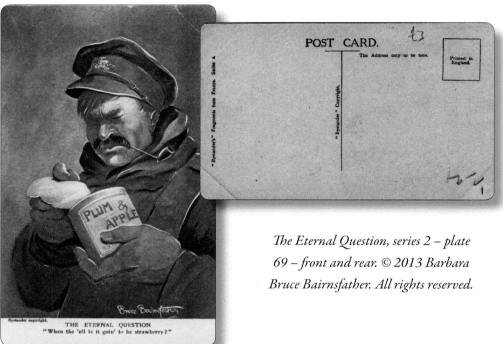

(No 2149) – plate 71.

Road, Biggleswade. "*Dear Miss Whitbread how are you all at Biggleswade. I received your last letter and am off to France in the morning. Will drop you a line when I get out. With kindest regards to all. Very sincerely Michael.*"

EVE gave man the Apple, but man made it ADAM sight worse by adding Plum to it! "Comique" series (No 2149) – plate 71.

On this McGill card, also sent in 1917, Billy tells Edith " . . . *we never get plum & apple. Will let you have a letter in a few days.*" – But it should be noted that Billy had not as yet left for the front.

'Into your Dug-out, Boys – there's a Shell bursting!' 'Comique' series (No 1709) – plate 72.

(No 1709) – plate 72.

This isn't half a 'windy' place!
Il y a plutôt de l'orage par ici!

The card was sent from Blackpool on 14 April 1917 to Miss J C Pepperdine, Walesby, Market Rasen, Lincolnshire. "*Sat morning. Dearest, getting on alright nothing said about being late back. It was a wash-out, not on draft yet, hope you are well love to all so ta ta. With love Diddy better weather here love to all at the farm.*"

This isn't half a 'windy' place! (Also in French) – 'Comique' series (No 1610) – plate 73 – not postally used.

(No 1610) – plate 73.

Many cards were sent from Blackpool and from a large number of training and holding camps around the country.

"MON, IT'S DANGEROUS TO BE ALIVE HERE!!" (Also in French) "THE FRONT" series (No 1223) – plate 74.

"MON, IT'S DANGEROUS TO
BE ALIVE HERE !!"
C'est rudement dangereux d'être vivant ici !

(No 1223) – plate 74.

`This McGill card, unfortunately not dated or postmarked, shows a Scotsman under fire. The fascination message on the reverse may well have been written in faltering English by a young French lady *"Vendredi soir. Very dear Gosse I have spoken to our Ma. – She is willing 'like Barkis' in D. Copperfield. You can write to your comrade and friend that he has his room rue Badineau when he will come at Bordeaux. And tell him also we shall be glad to know a good fellow like him. – goodnight, make <u>no imprudences</u>, be a good child . . . no! A good elector. Ma says she kisses you well. And I also. Old sister Germany   Nisse has written a good letter. It was Christmas eve. He was well and says he sends friendly words to the comrades and <u>Henri</u> particularly. A card from J Stemmilen on his way to Tunis with a view of Cette. Y.M."*

13. WAR BREAD AND RATIONING

At the start of hostilities, there was a rush to stock up on food, with those who could afford it buying large quantities of non-perishables, in particular sugar and tinned foods. There were many stories of food-hoarders: however, the panic abated within days and it was not until 1917 that food shortages became a severe problem.[26]

"Look, Jimmy! – He's one o' them food 'oarders!" 'Comique' Series (No 2396) – plate 75 – sent from Blackpool on August 6 1918. *". . . Having a fine time weather simply grand B.pool is packed . . ."*

(No 2396) – plate 75.   *(No 2390) – plate 76.*

I don't like these food hoarders. 'Comique' series (No 2390) – plate 76 – sent from Cricklewood NW2 on May 5 1918.
(It would seem that the cat's owner was also a food hoarder.)

In 1914, two-thirds of Britain's food, measured in calories, came from overseas. Once war was declared, German U-boats started to attack and sink Allied merchant ships, destroying vital supplies, which included meat, grain and sugar. At the beginning of February 1917, unrestricted submarine warfare against Allied shipping was continued with a vengeance and, as a result, there was a very real threat to Britain of starvation.[27]

I'm no slacker, but my pants are! 'Comique' series (No 2445) – plate 77 –sent from Pevensey, Sussex on September 9 1918.

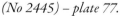

(No 2445) – plate 77.   *(No 2393) – plate 78.*

The scarcity of sugar forms the subject of a card in the 'Comique' series (No 2393) – plate 78 – sent on August 8 1918:
Gaze on it longingly,
Guard it with care.
You can't another lump
Any old where!

There's one thing about this rationing; we can make a fine pair of trousers for little Billy from where your stomach used to be! 'Comique' series (No 2430) – plate 79 – sent from Oxford on December 3 1918 shows the effect of rationing. Miss Giles is asked if she has escaped the flu. (Could this be the start of the 1919 influenza epidemic, which world-wide claimed more lives than the casualties of the First World War?)

(No 2430) – plate 79.

War-bread – from March 1917 onwards – was doctored. A higher proportion of raw wheat was used and other grains, like maize and barley, were mixed in; even potatoes were added. The new bread made the limited supplies go further and the loaves were more nutritious but they tasted unpleasant and were unpopular with the customer.[28] No longer was the British loaf pure white.

War Bred! 'Comique' series (No 2431) – plate 80 – sent from Forest Row, Sussex on October 25 1919. Miss D Terry, 7 New Stein Mansions, Brighton writes "*Dearest Daisy, Just a P.C. to let you know that I should like to come down on Tuesday and see you again if you can get out. We could meet at the same place and same time. Write and let me know if this is possible. Lots of love Yrs XXX Billy.*" Daisy may well have been in service and we can only wonder if their love blossomed.

(No 2431) – plate 80.

WAR BRED!

LITTLE TOM TUCKER CRIES FOR HIS SUPPER
WHAT SHALL WE GIVE HIM?
War Bread twelve hours old, (with 10 percent of Potato Flour) and
Margarine – then perhaps
HE WON'T CRY FOR IT SO MUCH TOMORROW NIGHT!
'Comique' series (No 2386) – plate 81 – sent on January 18 1919 to Miss
Maggie Nixon, 2 Railway Walk, Southport. "*. . . We have a letter from Ernie*
this morning. He says 50 men have got home. So I don't think he will be
long. . . ."

In December 1917, ration cards were distributed to 300,000 Birmingham families for tea, sugar, butter and margarine.[29] By February 1918, the Government had introduced a nationally co-ordinated scheme of food rationing and, by April, all of Britain was required to have meat rationing.[30] Every householder had to register with a retailer who supplied the appropriate ration goods – in particular sugar, butter, margarine and lard (which were all compulsorily rationed) and tea, cheese and jam (rationed according to the decisions of local food committees).[31]

Now everything you eat to-day
Is Government controlled,
And before you get your ration,
Your name must be enrolled.

But though controlled in food and drink
I swear by stars above,
They never can or will control
The soppy thing called Love!

(No 2386) – plate 81.

'Comique' series (No 2389) – plate 82 – sent by Will to Grace (no date or postmark) informs us that even if the Government can control rations, they cannot control (his) love.

(No 2389) – plate 82.

14. THEY ALSO SERVED – WOMAN'S WAR WORK AND WAR BONDS

O ne of the reasons for the introduction of rationing was that the Government was anxious to promote a sense of shared sacrifice in order to encourage the continued support of workers in the munitions industries. Women now played a vital role in Royal Ordnance Factories and national shell-filling factories, as well as in other engineering, metal-working and aircraft industries.[32]

WE'LL "DELIVER THE GOODS"
MORE MUNITIONS WANTED

YES, AN' IT AIN'T A BIT LIKE KNITTIN' SOCKS EITHER!!
On card no 282 – Plate 83 – in the TWO-EIGHT-ONE Series, sent on 23 August 1915 to Mrs Ross Junior, 53 Hallas Bar, Haleswood, Sheffield, Mum says, *"My dear Lizzie I expect I shall be meeting you doing something like this, they are starting a large munition place in Nottingham so look out . . ."*

(No 282) – plate 83.

NOTICE – ALL WORKERS ON MUNITIONS WILL WORK IN SHIFTS. "Well, I want to do my bit, but I draw the line at that!!" 'Comique' series (No 1784) – plate 84 – sent by Wilfred on 10 August 1917 to Miss A Botterill of Rugby. *"Dear Ada, Just a PC to let you know I am having a fine time. Weather till good I went & found Aunt yesterday but she was at work until 11 o'clock at night so of course I was not able to see her hope all are well Love Wilfred."* Presumably Wilfred's aunt was on the late shift.

NOTICE – NIGHT SHIFTS MUST RESUME THEIR DUTIES PROMPTLY AT 8 O'CLOCK. I hate working in a night shift! 'Comique' series (No 2190) – plate 85 – not postally used.

(No 1784) – plate 84.

(No 2190) – plate 85.

The British people also showed resolve in the vital role of financing the war. They had already contributed much in the new direct income tax and in a range of indirect taxes, principally on drink and tobacco. Now, with renewed vigour, they invested yet more money in war bonds and loans. Between October 1917 and September 1918, war bonds raised a staggering £1,000 million.[33]

BUY NATIONAL WAR BONDS NOW. *MAN POWER – that's what's goin' to win this blinkin' war!* 'Comique' series (No 2412) – plate 86 – sent by Arthur on 6 September 1918 to Miss R Harding, Tuffley, Gloucester.

(No 2412) – plate 86.

IF YOU CANNOT FIGHT LEND YOUR MONEY 'Comique' series (No 1546) – plate 87 – not dated or postmarked.

(No 1546) – plate 87.

Don't be Stingy! 'Comique' series (No 1475) – plate 88 – postmark illegible.

(No 1475) – plate 88.

"EVERYBODY SEEMS TO BE MAKIN' SACRIFICES – 'CEPT ME. I – I – I'LL WASH MY NECK TOMORROW!!" TWO-EIGHT-ONE series (No 281) – plate 89 – sent on 8 October 1915. McGill's little boy evidently has no money to give to the Red Cross or the Belgian Refugees and he is too young to drink alcohol or join the army. What can he do to help the war effort?

(No 281) – plate 89.

15. AIR RAIDS BY ZEPPELINS

Zeppelins came to symbolise German technology and prowess in the first years of WWI, before an adequate response was formulated to combat such raids and the first of the airships was shot down. The advantage of Zeppelins was in sowing fear and anxiety in the civil population. However, the number of Zeppelin raids was in fact few – just over fifty in over forty-five months.

At the outbreak of war, a total of eleven Zeppelins were in operation and the first raid over British soil took place on 19 January 1915. There were a further twenty-six attacks in 1915, accounting for just over half of all Zeppelin raids in the war. The first raid over London was on 31 May 1915.[34]

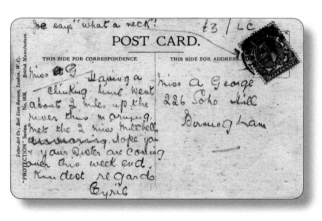

(No 1038) – plate 90 – front and reverse.

WE'RE PREPARED FOR ZEPPELIN RAIDS!! 'Protection' series (No 1038) – plate 90 – sent from Evesham on 23 August 1915. To Miss A George, 226 Soho Hill, Birmingham *"Miss G – Having a clicking time Went about 2 miles up the river this morning. Met the 2 Miss Mitchells. Hope you & your sister are coming over this weekend Kindest regards Cyril. Joe says 'What a neck!'"*

On a card in the "TWO – O – THREE" series (No 208), not dated or postmarked, Jim writes "*Dear Harry, Just a line hoping that you and all at home are in the best of health as it leaves me at present. I heard that you have had another Zep raid and all had a rare fright. Whenever are they going to bring one down to put a stop to them. Will you remember me to Edgar Toney and the others at the wharf. I will send him a few lines as soon as I can. No more this time. My best regards to you and Edie, Ernest and aunt. Jim.*" This card was probably sent in an envelope from France as the caption is written in both English and French and before September 1916, when the first Zeppelin was shot down.

The random nature of the attacks led to Heath Robinson style air-raid warnings. "A policeman came round on a bicycle with a notice on him saying 'Take cover' and ringing his bicycle bell."[35]

AIR RAID TAKE COVER. 'Comique' series (No 2194) – plate 91 – not postally used.

(No 2194) – plate 91 – front and reverse.

"WHY DON'T I STEER? 'OW CAN I? D'YER THINK THIS IS A BALLY ZEPPELIN??"
"TWO-EIGHT-ONE" series (No 290) – plate 92 – sent from Manchester on 17
August 1916 by J T Hills to Mr H Meadowcroft, Colwyn Bay, North Wales. "

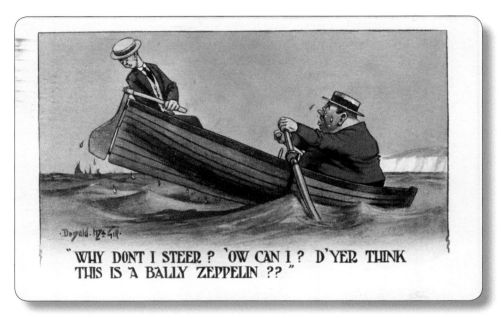

(No 290) – plate 92

For eighteen months, the German air-ships had bombed Britain with seeming
impunity, but in September 1916 this unlimited success ended dramatically.
The first air-ship to be shot down over England was SL11, attacked by
Lieutenant William Leef Robinson, who machine-gunned SL11 with the
new incendiary bullets, setting it alight.[36] By the end of 1916, the Zeppelin
had had its day as an effective weapon, with senior German officers tacitly
admitting that raids over Britain by air-ship had become impossible. Over
400 crewmen had died, or around 40 percent of all those who served in the
air-ships. Between the first Zeppelin raid in January 1915 and the last raid in
August 1918, only 556 people were killed as a direct result of their bombs, or
fewer than three people a week.[37]

16. AIR-RAIDS BY AEROPLANES

During the second half of the war, the German bomber aircraft, the Gotha IV, operated from airfields in Belgium, mostly in the area around Ghent, and attacked London and the Home Counties east of the capital. Although the Goth IV had a range of over 400 miles and delivered over 1,100 pound bombs, few raids could be carried out successfully further to the west. The British airfields were also to be found around London and close to the coast in Kent and Essex.[38]

NOTICE! IN VIEW OF POSSIBLE RAIDS (BY) HOSTILE AIRCRAFT ALL LIGHTS MUST BE LOWERED. Even the War has its advantages. "TWO-SIX-THREE" series (No 265) – plate 93 – sent on 22 April 1916 to 9507 Sergt. J J Goodge, B Comp. 9th Lincoln Regt. Bracton Camp, Cannock Chase, Staffordshire, Isabel writes "*I suppose this is the sort of thing that takes place Saturday night in Stafford.*"

(No 265) – plate 93.

(No 1991) – plate 94.

Somebody knows! Somebody cares! 'Comique' series (No 1991) – plate 94 – sent by Jimmy to Ethel, Dol and Norah White, 208 Bohemia Rod, St Leonards (on) Sea on 29 August 1918. Jimmy has drawn an aeroplane and written *To DOL / MIND NOBODY IS LOOKING FROM ABOVE.*

17. THE NAVY – WAR AT SEA

Essentially, the war at sea was one of blockades: both sides were trying to block essential overseas supplies of food and raw materials from reaching the enemy.

Germany tried to break the blockade by sailing its fleet past the British fleet out into the Atlantic. These attempts culminated in the Battle of Jutland in May 1916, where the British suffered greater losses but succeeded in driving the Germans back into port.

After Jutland, the Germans relied on submarines (the U-boats) and mines to disrupt the Allied supply lines. However, they attacked all shipping indiscriminately and this tactic resulted in the United States joining the war in April 1917. By 1918, this support and improved use of convoys and antisubmarine weapons meant that the power of the U-boats was destroyed.

WE'RE BOUND TO COME OUT ON TOP! Also in French. "FIRST LINE" series (No 1347) – plate 95 – not dated or postmarked.

(No 1347) – plate 95.

"Dear Annie, I have just received Raly letter and the PO for 10/- Thank you for the same. You do not loose much time in sending what I want love, wish that you could just be out here for a week Now little Scottie is here he makes us all laugh, I am your loving Husband XXXX Joe."

"THEY PARTED ON THE SHORE" FIRST LINE series (No 1354) – plate 96 – sent from Devonport on 6 August 1916 to Miss Bastone, South Tarn House, Dartmouth: *"Dear Annie, How do you liked this? A German submarine has been seen near Plymouth Sound last night and it makes one shake. Hope you did not have much of a rush at the Vic. Hope you are not working too hard. Frank F."*

(No 1354) – plate 96 – front and reverse.

What's in a name, anyway? 'Comique' series (No 2008) – plate 97 – dated 24 June – and sent via the censor by Bob (who is on active service) from Mess 2, HMS Raider, to Mrs W Y Stevenson, Kingsdown Avenue, South Croydon, Surrey. The card was passed by the censor. *"Dear Mum & Dad, I have had John Bull tonight. You remember when I was on leave you proposed something. Well a suitable time may be in a week or two. I don't think there is anything else to tell you tonight. Bob XXXXX"* What was proposed?

(No 2008) – plate 97 – front and reverse.

<u>H.M.S. Raider</u> – R class destroyer, commissioned in October 1916 for service with the Grand Fleet.

McGill's cards, which before the war had been printed in Saxony in Germany, now proclaimed 'British Production' or 'British Manufacture Throughout'.

We've got "some" guns on our ship! 'Comique' series (No 2007) – plate 98 – sent on 29 April 1918 from Plymouth to Mrs J Slee, Skewen, Nr Neath, South Wales.

We've got "some" guns on our ship!

"Dear M, D & C Bound for Rosyth Scotland in morning don't worry feeling A1. Don't mention about ship when writing best love Reg XXXXX busy getting ready."

(No 2007) – plate 98

"Aint I never goin' to have a chance of killin' a Hun? (Also in French) 'Comique' series (No 1470) – plate 99 – sent from Dover on 19 September 1918 by Auntie Georgie to Master Teddie Blake, 40 Worlpole Road, Isleworth, Middx. *"Dear Teddie Just a PC because I forgot to send you one on your birthday. I hope you are keeping a good boy. Best love from Auntie Georgie."*

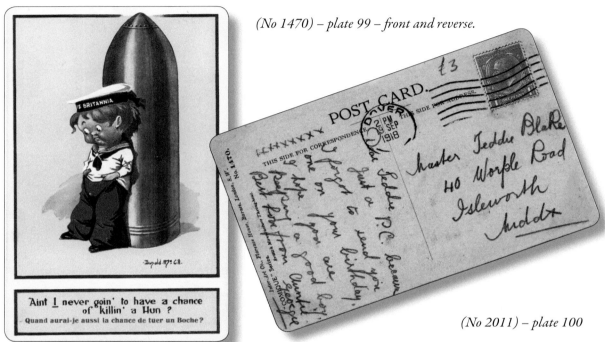

(No 1470) – plate 99 – front and reverse.

(No 2011) – plate 100

There were even suggestions that children were disappointed that the war might be over before they were old enough to fight. McGill was quick to portray the perils caused to Allied shipping by both submarines and mines.

The Sailor's Dream. "The sea, the sea, the open sea!" (Also in French). 'Comique' series (No 2011) – plate 100 – not postmarked, but dated September 1918 and sent from France (B.E.F.) *"Dear old Jack, Thanks for your letter of Sept 3. Very pleased to hear you are OK. Have you had the sensation pictured on the other side. I hope you have a good time at home."*

MINES IN THE NORTH SEA. "MINE'S HERE." "TWENTY-SIXTY-EIGHT" Series (No 1269) – plate 101 – sent via the censor on 13 October 1917 to Miss P Cripps in Tuffley, near Gloucester.

(No 1269) – plate 101

Frequently, sailors had to give their address as "H.M.S. –, c/o G.P.O. London" as portrayed on card no 2010 in the 'Comique' series – plate 102 – which was sent from Harwich on 4 February 1918.

A pre-war card, no 1468, published by Asher and sent on 7 June 1915 by Charlie from H.M.S. Lowestoft c/o G.P.O. London to Mr John Clearle, 9 Engine Lane, Beggarlee, Newthorpe, Notts., England – *"Dear Jack, I received your letter last night, also received paper this morning. I received a letter from W Wilkinson this morning and he says that he may get home shortly. Just remember me to Sam Cliff if he comes home. There was £2-0-0 remitted home in Dad's name on the first of the month. I am sorry to hear that Uncle Tom had his finger end taken off. Am pleased to hear that Eddy is getting better. Will write letter in a day or two if not at sea. I am going on alright. Please remember me to all. With love to all I remain your loving Brother Charlie."*

(No 2010) – plate 102

H.M.S. Lowestoft was part of the Harwich Force which made a sweep into Heligoland Bight on 28 August 1914, tempting the German forces on to the guns of the British battle-cruisers under the command of Admiral David Beatty. The plot was successful – three German cruisers were sunk – Ariadne, Köln and Mainz and the destroyer V187. HMS *Lowestoft* joined the 2nd Light Cruiser Squadron 1915–1916.

An Asher card A1186, dated 11 September 1915 and sent to Mr A G Mitchell, (No 461) 20 Mess, H.M.S. *Marlborough*, 1st Battle Squadron, c/o G.P.O. London "*My dear brother Just a card, hoping same will find you as it leaves me at present. I will write a letter later as I am so awfully busy. If you see Will & Leslie give them my best respects. With fondest love from Eddie XXXX.*" If A G Mitchell was a sailor, what was his rank?

18. MOCKING THE ENEMY

Anti-German attitudes were driven largely by the newspapers of the day. One of the most notorious, John Bull, regularly sold between one and two million copies an issue and warned the public against the enemy within, namely "the Hun".[39] As a result, everything associated with Germany was attacked or rejected by many people. Dachshunds were kicked or abused in the street, German shepherd dogs were re-designated Alsatians, German measles was re-named "Belgian Flush" and traditional German sausages and sauerkraut were suddenly anglicised.[40]

MORE GERMAN ATROCITIES – Series not stated – (no 935) – plate 103 – not postally used.

(No 935) – plate 103

After war was declared, McGill drew cartoons depicting the Kaiser and his son, Little Willie, and German soldiers depicting them as objects of ridicule. The Allies, however, were depicted as brave and caring, even for the foe.

A D ------ ROTTEN PEAR! TWO EIGHT ONE series – (no 287) – plate 104 – not postally used.

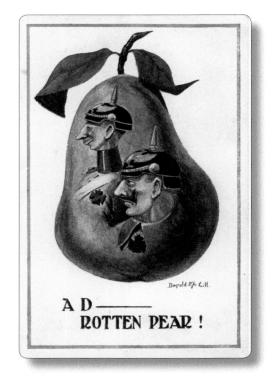

(No 287) – plate 104

(No 1996) – plate 105

Well, I'm blowed, and I only called 'im "Little Willie"! – also in French – 'Comique' series – (no 1996) – plate 105 – dated 4 December 1918. Possibly sent from the village of Vervicque in France by Charlie, who sends no further message.

"SAFETY FIRST!" – TWELVE SIX EIGHT series – (no 1271) – plate 106 – not dated or postmarked. Sent to Master C Wyatt, 116 Alan Road, Ipswich. Suffolk. *"Dear C, Just a P Card hope you and Mum are quite well as it leaves me alright at present. I have not received any letters since Friday. Best love to all from Dad XXXXX "*

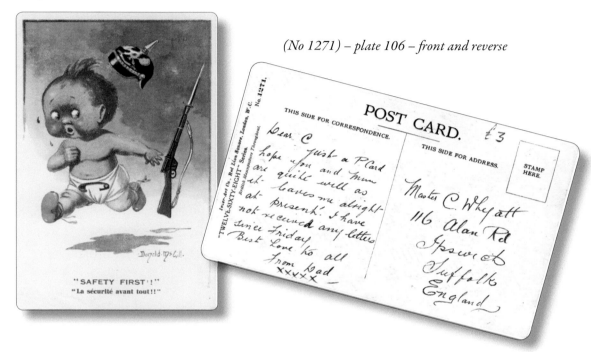

(No 1271) – plate 106 – front and reverse

"IT'S A WAY WE HAVE IN THE ARMY" – 'Comique' series – (No 1700) – plate 107 – sent on 28 June 1917 from Macclesfield to Mrs F Roberts, c/o Mrs Entwhistle, Argyl House, 79 Coronation Street, corner of Hull Road, Blackpool. *"Polly – I am just writing this card and it is raining here. I think you are all having a good time. I think you are busy with the soldier boys. Next time you write put a stamp on. I think you was too busy with the boys."* Large numbers of soldiers were billeted in the Blackpool area at this time.

(No 1700) – plate 107

19. CARDS AND LETTERS HOME

Both when in training or at the Front, soldiers and sailors sent letters to, and hoped to receive letters from, their families and loved ones. Many messages were sent as letters, others as postcards. All those sent from the Front had to be passed by the censor, usually a junior officer. A blue pencil was used to strike through offending passages, including the location from which the card or letter was sent. The original censor stamps taken with the B.E.F. in 1914 were small red circular handstamps. At the end of the year, because so many had been lost during the retreat, they were replaced with a square handstamp. Not surprisingly, both of these marks are rare.

A card or letter enclosed in an envelope was sent via the censor on 28 December 1914 to Messrs Bastian Electric Heating Syndicate Ltd in London. The address was corrected and the sender stated that 'no stamp available'. This was not a problem as stamps were not required on letters or cards sent by men on active service.

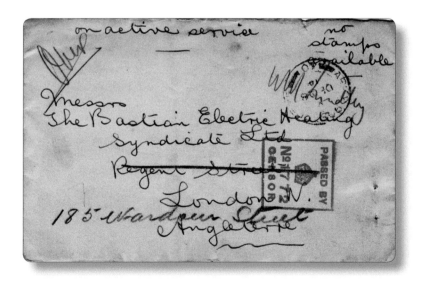

The triangle, used in 1915, is less rare. In January 1916, the triangle was replaced with a hexagonal stamp. In November 1916, the hexagon was replaced with an oval and this was replaced in turn with a rectangular handstamp in October 1917. This was used until the end of the war. It should be noted that the above information applies only to the Western Front. Shield-shaped stamps were used in Italy. In Solenica (now Thessalonki) in Greece an octagonal handstamp was used. A few rectangular handstamps are found on cards dated 1919 and even on some cards dated 1920, examples of which can be found on page 117.

At the start of hostilities, not all the action was on the Western Front. Two cards posted on the same day, 14 August 1915, bear square handstamps and the signature of R Loder, the Censor. As they feature local views, PORT SAID, STREET OF THE COMMERCE and PORT SAID, STREET OF FRANCIS-JOSEPH, it is most likely that they were sent from Port Said by a soldier to his wife, Mrs Askew, 81 Queen's Road, East Grinstead, Sussex. (card 1) *"My own dear wife, Well, just a few more lines hoping you are well and getting on alright. These are a few P.C.'s where we are now Have been here for a few days but shall soon be moving again. Please to say that I am well and waiting to hear from you soon."* (Card 2) *"Well, my duck, I can't say much about our doings yet. Will tell you more later and what a lot I shall have to tell you when I return again which I hope won't be long. Am always thinking of you only. XXXX"*

The Suez Canal was a crucial waterway which had to be defended at all costs and this entailed a considerable military commitment to prevent any hostile incursion or possible sabotage by the Turks. Troops sent to defend the Canal included Territorials of the British 42nd Division and the 10th and 11th Indian Divisions, joined later by the ANZAC Corps.[41]

Naval censor handstamps were different from those used by the Army. Examples seen include a large circle with 'Passed by Censor' in the centre, used on 19 December 1916; a large rectangular handstamp, again stating 'Passed by Censor' and used on 15 April 1917; and a small purple circle with 'Passed by Censor' and a crown inside – this last one was probably used in 1918.

A card passed by the Army censor and sent on 4 September 1916 to Miss E Brandon, 21 Hetley Road, Shepherds Bush, London W. *"Dear Edi, Just a card to wish you many happy returns of the 6th. This is one of the cards left from my recent 'holiday' of which I still retain many jolly memories. Should like to be running over for another game of ping. pong. – It's a quieter game than the one we're accustomed to play out here. Old Fritz has a knack of "feuding" with the sort of balls that hurt when they hit. You ought to see this war – up on yonder ridge as I write. No fun. With fondest regards, Yours, Les."*

"ONE-SIX-ONE" series (No 165) – Plate 109 – not postally used.

(No 165) – plate 109 – front and reverse

"I hope the Censor didn't read this!" (Also in French).

To make the work less demanding, cards were produced which only required the sender to cross out what was not applicable.

At least one McGill card mentions these Field Service cards. *"Only a measley Field Postcard again. I believe he's keeping another dog!"* (Also in French) 'Comique' series (No 2673) – plate 110 – sent on 1 April 1919.

(No 2673) – plate 110

On 11 July 1917, a Field Service postcard was sent to Mrs W Stringer, High Street, Limpsfield, Surrey, by Private Harry William Stringer (T/201297) of the 7th Battalion, The Queen's Royal West Surrey Regiment. Harry Stringer was later killed in action and the date of his death is given as 24 October 1918, just 18 days before the end of hostilities. Harry has no known grave but is commemorated on Panel 3, Vis-en-Artois Memorial, France.[42] See plates 111 and 112.

Plate 111

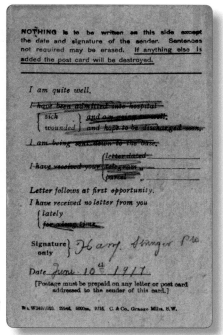

Plate 112

Another Field Service postcard was passed by the Censor and posted on 1 November 1914 to L Nicholson Esq., 822 Gladys Avenue, Los Angeles, California (USA) via England. Ned informs Mr Nicholson that "I am quite well. Letter follows at first opportunity. I have received no letter from you lately. Ned. Oct. 31. 1914."

This card is interesting for a number of reasons. The Censor's stamp is the rare small red circle used in 1914; the card was sent to an address in America; and it is possible that Ned was an American fighting alongside the British before America entered the war in April 1917.

Postcards were often sent enclosed in an envelope. Some were dated but they did not have a postmark. The obvious advantage of enclosing a postcard in an envelope was that there was more room for the message and, although censored, a little more privacy. The majority of letters and postcards from the Front were written in pencil but not necessarily from the trenches but rather when the soldiers were resting or on standby and behind the front lines.

However, Albert 'Smiler' Marshall', quoted in *Last Post*, stressed the problems faced when writing from the Front. *"We used to try and write letters home but oh crikey say that you've got an envelope and a writing pad – well, it poured with rain and it got soaking wet and that was no good. Even if you managed to write – well, you couldn't stick it all down because it had to be censored by the officer."*[43]

By no means all the cards sent from the front were those drawn by McGill. Many local views found their way to British homes. If the card had the name of a local town or village displayed on the photograph, it was usually erased by the censor.

A card showing a French village scene had the location erased by the Censor. The sender, Lance-Sergeant J E Johnston, wrote on 17 February 1915 via the Field Post Office and the Censor to Mrs Johnston, Clonmell Road, Tottenham, London N, with many requests. *"Herewith is a photo of a French family. Don't forget my cake. Don't forget packing also underwear and socks. Nothing else in the way of clothes. Fine & cold weather. Best of love to all from Tom. L/Sgt J E Johnston. Should like a pair of 'cork' soles (socks) 10s."*

THE SUN IS BRIGHT, THE BREEZE IS SOFT
THE SEA AND SKY ARE BLUE
THERE'S ONLY JUST ONE THING I WANT
AND THAT'S A LINE FROM YOU.

(No A1282) – dated 6 September 1916. (This is an Asher card printed pre-war.) *"Dear Bro. I seem a long time since I here from you as I am used to seeing the letters you send home. You will have heard we are at Blackpool.*

I wish you was with us but never mind we are crowded here with soldiers. We have been to the Loos Trenches. Here they are at the south end where wounded soldiers are. They take us round and explain things to us. We are going to the hospital tomorrow. There are 2,500 wounded soldiers in. So no more at present. Hoping you are alright. Your ever loving Bro."

The Loos Trenches were a tourist attraction set up in the dunes of Lytham St Anne's, just south of Blackpool. With front-line and communication trenches, fire bays and traverses and many other aspects of current military architecture, these trenches were intended to provide some sense of trench life for the visitor.[44]

I LOVE TO BE A SAILOR – A card in the "Artistique Songs" series (No 2090) not dated or postmarked. *"Dear Mother, I am writing this in the sentry box on guard, hoping it finds you all quite well and happy as I am alright yet, I received your parcel yesterday also the papers. Well dear Mother I won't be long before I see you as the officer letting us all have a leaf (sic) in turns. So he alright as he is one of our own Reg."*

I've put on two stone since I joined! (Also in French) 'Comique' series (No 1466) – Plate 113 – sent by George from Seaford, Sussex, on 1 November 1916, to Mrs G Spinks, 38 Thorngrove Road, Upton Park, London. *"Excuse card I have put notepaper away. Dear Kate, In Y.M.C.A. here for the last time. Thought I would let you know am moving from here 2am in the morning (Wednesday). Will be up all night. Shall arrive at Luton about 10 or 11. Will write as soon as possible. Love to you and boys, George."* Y.M.C.A. huts provided basic comforts, shelter and a place for recreation for soldiers, both at home and in wooden huts in rest areas close to

I've put on two stone since I joined !

"J'ai augmenté de dix Kilos depuis que je suis soldat!"

(No 1466) – plate 113

the front. Postcards and stationary could be purchased and cards and letters written in comparative comfort. George may well have written his postcard while seated at a table in the Seaford Camp Y.M.C.A. hut. Photographic cards, showing men at the front, were issued by the Y.M.C.A. to raise funds for their huts.

She's the sort of Girl that's <u>worth fightin'</u> for! (Also in French) 'Comique' series (No 1716) – plate 114 – sent on 26 May 1917 via the censor to Master Jim Morris, North Road, Largs, Scotland by his Uncle Arthur. *"Dear Jim, Father and I were together and had a stroll along the Battlefield. Uncle Arthur."*

(No 1716) – plate 114   *(No 1486) – plate 115*

Some messages were brief but no less heartfelt:
WE'RE MAKING OUR GRUB GO A LONG WAY HERE (Also in French) 'Comique' series (No 1486) – plate 115 – no date or postmark.
 "To my Beloved Wife with fondest love and best wishes from your loving hubby Jack."

A message written on the back of a card (Plate 34) reads *"Dear Frankie, That picture was the best you have done. I have hung it up over my bed and all the men think it is great. Dad."*

From two loving hearts you've left behind. Children are shown to be missing their fathers and pet dogs their masters. 'Comique' series (No 1787) – plate 116 – not postally used.

(No 1787) – plate 116   *(No 1465) – plate 117*

"Some Dad, mine!!" (Also in French) 'Comique' series (No 1465) – plate 117 – written on 6 September but posted via the Army post office and the censor on 14 September 1917 to Miss Winnie Cook, 21 Canon Road, Bromley, Kent. *"Dear Winnie, Tell Mum that I am well & hope you are all the same. Hope you like being back at school again now. Goodbye – love to you all from Daddy XXXXX"*.

– ' – an' watch over my dear Dad!' 'Comique' series (No 2566), not dated or postmarked – plate 118 – sent to Master L F Lord, Seawards End, Saffron Walden, Essex, *"With best wishes from Grandad & Granny for a happy birthday."*

That's where Dad is! (Also in French). 'Comique' series (No 1618) – plate 119 -– sent on 23 January 1918 via the censor to Master E J Hinton, 8 Goldstone Road, Hove, Brighton, England. *"Hope you are better now. Thanks for your letter. Much love Daddy."*

(No 2566) – plate 118

(No 1618) – plate 119

YOU'RE MY GREAT, BIG, WONDERFUL BABY (Also in French). 'Comique' series (No 1986) – plate 120 – not dated or postmarked.

"Dear Ruth, Thanks for p.cards. Hope you are alright. How is Jack & chickens & rabbits & all the rest of the family? Love from Frank XXXX."

A number of cards drawn by McGill requested the recipient to write to their soldier-boy. As the cards do not have a translation in French under the caption written in English, they were most probably sold in the U.K. and not sent home by soldiers at the Front. However, the message is clear – a card or letter from home is vital to raise the morale of those serving overseas.

(No 1986) – plate 120

(No 2128) – plate 121

RIGHT TURN And don't forget that it's YOUR TURN to write.
'Comique' series (No 2128) – plate 121 – not postally used.

IF ONLY YOU WERE HERE!
If only you were here to-day
Instead of being far away
I'd whisper loving words & true
Instead – I send this card to you.

"I 2 U" series (No 1045) – plate
122 – sent on 30 August 1915 to
Miss Luckett c/o Mrs Abrahams, The
Towers, Clacton-on-Sea, Essex.

(No 1045) – plate 122

(No 2275) – plate 123

WHEN THIS YOU SEE –
REMEMBER ME!
'Comique' series (No 2275) –
plate 123 – sent on 9 August 1918.

20. SONGS ON POSTCARDS

McGill lost no time promoting war songs on his postcards. Examples include "Are we downhearted? No!". This upbeat verse, often belted out by a platoon of marching soldiers, became one of the most popular rallying cries of WWI.

Are we downhearted? – No!
Then let your voices ring,
And altogether sing.
Are we downhearted? – No!

"ARE WE DOWN-HEARTED? NO-O-O-O-O-O-O-!!" "Patriotic" series IV (No 817) – plate 124 – not dated or postmarked but probably sent in 1915 to 8460 Pte. H Foulkes. *"Dear Harry, Just a line to tell you that we are alright. I hope you are the same. Harry – are we downhearted? No-o-o-o-o-o!"*

The words of "I wonder who's kissing her now?", which were first introduced in 1909 in the musical "The Prince of Tonight", also hinted at the problems of being parted from a loved one, either a sweetheart left at home or the soldier serving overseas. *I WONDER WHO'S KISSING HER NOW?"* "TWELVE-SEVEN-FOUR" series (No 1278) – plate 125 – date not legible, sent by Dolly, possibly from Hertford, to her Aunt Alice, Miss A Scott, c/o Mrs J Scott, Carleton Rode, nr Attleborough, Norfolk. *"My Dear Auntie, Alice thought you would like a few lines from me.*

(No 817) – plate 124

(No 1278) – plate 125

Hope you are quite well as it leaves us all at present. I am thinking of you today. Wish I was with you in the meadows. Give my love to dear Granny – tell her to keep smiling as I am sometimes. We have had no raid since we have been home. Now dear give my love to all – your ever-loving little niece, Dolly XXXX".

Art thou weary art thou languid? 'Comique' series (No 1661) – plate 126 – sent by Dick on 8 May 1917 from Plymouth, Devon, to Miss D Birch, also of Plymouth. *"Dear D, I am going on leave to night so I shan't be able to see you to morrow but if I am back and able to get out Sunday will look out for you on the Hoe. Will sends his best wishes to your friend. Yours, Dick".*

(No 1661) – plate 126

"Pack up your troubles in your old kit-bag, and Smile! Smile, Smile!"
'Comique' series (No 2002) – plate 127 – sent on 30 November 1917 from
Aldershot by Miss West (Patty) to Miss W Whincop, Top Munitions Works,
Munitions Works, Leiston, Suffolk. *"Dear Molly, Just a card as promised.
Having a lovely time Love Miss West (Patty)."* Molly may well have been
working in shifts (see plates 71 and 72).

(No 2002) – plate 127

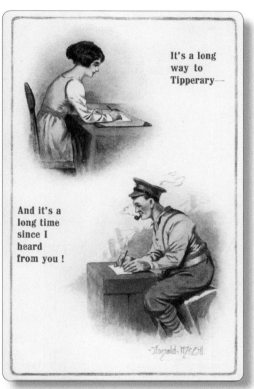

(No 2281) – plate 128

"It's a long way to Tipperary" was first introduced by the 2nd Battalion,
Connaught Rangers, an Irish regiment stationed in Tipperary before the
war. They sang as they disembarked in France on 13 August 1914 and its
jaunt rhythm immediately caught on with troops of other Allied regiments.[45]
It's a long way to Tipperary – and it's a long time since I heard from you!
'Comique' series (No 2281) – plate 128 – not postally used.

21. RACISM IN THE TRENCHES

There was a time when George Blackman would have done anything for the mother country. In 1914, in a flush of youth and patriotism, he told the recruiting officer he was 18 – he was actually 17 – and joined the British West Indies Regiment.

"Lord Kitchener said with the black race, he could whip the world," Blackman recalls. "We sang songs: 'Run Kaiser William, run for your life, boy'." He closes his eyes as he sings, and keeps them closed for the rest of our interview. "We wanted to go. The island government told us the king said all Englishmen must go to join the war. The country called all of us."

Enthusiasm for the battle was widespread across the Caribbean. While some declared it a white man's war, leaders and thinkers such as the Jamaican Marcus Garvey said young men from the islands should fight in order to prove their loyalty and to be treated as equals. The islands donated £60m in today's money to the war effort – cash they could ill afford.

While Kitchener's private attitude was that black soldiers should never be allowed at the front alongside white soldiers, the enormous losses – and the interference of George V – made it inevitable. Although Indian soldiers had been briefly in the trenches in 1914 and 1915, Caribbean troops did not arrive until 1915.

When they arrived, they often found that fighting was to be done by white soldiers only – black soldiers were assigned the dirty, dangerous jobs of loading ammunition, laying telephone wires and digging trenches. Conditions were appalling. Blackman rolls up his sleeve to show me his armpit: "It was cold. And everywhere there were white lice. We had to shave the hair there because the lice grow there. All our socks were full of white lice."

A poem written by an anonymous trooper, entitled *The Black Soldier's Lament,* showed how bitter the disappointment was:

Stripped to the waist and sweated chest
Midday's reprieve brings much-needed rest
From trenches deep toward the sky.
Non-fighting troops and yet we die.

Yet there is evidence that some Caribbean soldiers were involved in actual combat in France. Photographs from the time show black soldiers armed with British Lee Enfield rifles, and there are reports of West Indies Regiment soldiers fighting off counter-attacks – one account tells how a group fought off a German assault armed only with knives they had brought from home. Blackman still remembers trench fights he fought in, alongside white soldiers.

"They called us darkies," he says, recalling the casual racism of the time. "But when the battle starts, it didn't make a difference. We were all the same. When you're there, you don't care about anything. Every man there is under the rifle."

He remembers one attack with particular clarity. "The Tommies said: 'Darkie, let them have it.' I made the order: 'Bayonets, fix' and then 'B company, fire'. You know what it is to go and fight somebody hand to hand? You need plenty nerves. You push that bayonet in there and hit with the butt of the gun – if he is dead he is dead, if he live he live."

The West Indies Regiment experienced racism from the Germans as well as the British. "The Tommies, they brought up some German prisoners and these prisoners were spitting on their hands and wiping on their faces, to say we were painted black," says Blackman.

He didn't make friends. "Don't have no friend. A soldier don't got friends. Know why? You believe that you are dead now. Your friend is this: the gun. That is your friend."

• *Extracted from an interview by Simon Rogers first published in the*
Guardian *on November 6 2002.*

During the First World War, there was racism in the Army. This fact is well supported by the interview in 2002 of George Blackman by Simon Rogers. However, the McGill card is difficult to interpret. The drawing was finished towards the end of hostilities or perhaps after peace was declared and so the fact that conscription was extended to married men in April 1916 would indicate the proposed marriage would do little to prevent the coloured man being sent to the front. Also there is much evidence to support the fact that coloured men were discouraged form enlisting and, if they did enlist, were prevented from fighting alongside white soldiers. It is unlikely the card was drawn to encourage coloured men to enlist or to portray those who did not as cowards.

"No, Sir, I ain't getting' mayried to keep out ob de army. Is two good reasons. One is, I's all mused up in love, an' the other I's just naturally scared to death of them there Germans!"
'Comique' series (No 2328) – plate 129 – sent to Miss Pike, Woodrow Farm, Uffculme, Devon on 24 ? 1919. No correspondence on the card, only the address. Postmark only partially visible; possibly sent from Honiton.

(No 2328) – plate 129

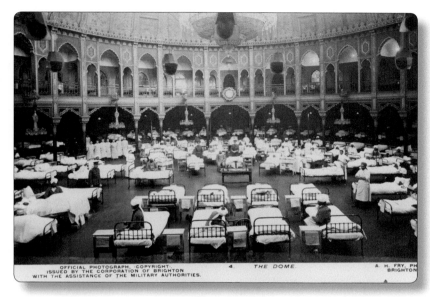

Plate 130

Indian soldiers did fight on behalf of the mother country in 1914 and 1915 and many of those who were wounded were treated in Brighton in the Royal Pavilion.

The Dome – plate 130 – and the Music Room, Royal Pavilion, Brighton – plate 131.

Plate 131

22. THE END IN SIGHT!

THE END IN SIGHT! 'Comique' series (No 1806) – plate 132 – sent from Forest Row 26 May 1917 (still 18 months to go!) to Master W Shaw, 129 Queen's Road, Dalston, London N:

"Dear William just a line hoping this will find you in better health and that you will get alright quick Dad."

(No 1806) – plate 132

"Here's one that's glad the war is over!"
'Comique' series (No 2642) – plate
133 – sent from Lewisham SE (London)
on 17 May 1919 to Mrs D Wragg in
Liverpool *"Eunice arrived safely. We
both wish you Many Happy Returns
Yours Willie."* In 1914 there were over
five million women in employment,
but more than twice as many did not
work. Many of these women turned to
knitting, with apparently unbounded
zeal. They knitted scarves, gloves,
waistcoats and socks, on the beach, on
trains, on trams, in the theatres and in
parks.[46]

*"Please can you tell me the way to
Agnes Weston's home? – - - - -*
'Comique' series (No 1969) O.A.S.
Army Post Office passed by Censor 14
November 1918 to Mrs Webb, 24 Morley
Avenue, Wood Green, N. London,
England. Card dated October 11.
(This could well be in error as the war
was not over in October. Also, the card
was postally used on 14 November 1918.)

(No 2642) – plate 133

*"To all – at last the happy day has arrived – 'Peace my God' it makes one
feel so happy I've received two letters which I will answer later. I hope you
are all O.K. Cas (?) I hope is better I am in the pink. I wish I were with you
now unfortunately I'm on guard tonight just my luck. Well cheer up! Best of
love yours Bill. Have the Guinness Ma?"*

23. DEMOBILISATION

There was dissatisfaction with the slow rate of demobilisation and, ten months after the Armistice, one million men remained in uniform while in February 1920 there were still 125,000 awaiting their return to civilian life.[47]

"Blow the War anyhow! Ma says she cant buy me a little brother till Father comes back from the Front!!" 'Comique' series (No 1652) – plate 134 – sent on 26 January 1919 from Kantara, Egypt, to Mrs D G M Moffatt, 147 Upper Conduit Street, Leicester. *"Poor little boy he will be a father himself if he has to wait till his father is demobilised before his mother will be able to buy him a baby. Fondest love Dave XXXXXX"*

(No 1652) – plate 134   (No 1662) – plate 135

"Young man, would you mind putting a cork in the spout in case it goes off?" 'Comique' series (No 1662) – plate 135 – sent from Sittingbourne 10 March 1919 to Mrs Thurmen, Bracknell, Berkshire *"Sittingbourne Monday:*

Dear Mum just a line to let you know I am here alright and that my demob is alright; am waiting to be sent to a dispersal station now so may be home by the weekend but don't know, I will let you know my address as soon as I have one, we are in billets for sleeping only. I hope Nan got home safe and that you are all well. I'm impatient to be out of this now I have started. Love from Bob." Is Bob on his way home after demob?

A card, no 2673, in the 'Comique' series, see plate 110, was posted from Blandford Camp, Blandford, Dorset on 1 April 1919 and sent by Will to his mother, Mrs C B Smethurst, Rising Brook, Stafford. *"Dearest mother, This is the last card you will get from me while I am in the Army, and a – - good job too. I wonder if this is what you thought when you had F.Cds [Field postcards]. Love from Will – Shall be home before you get this."*

A card showing a local view – the seafront at Whimereux, just south of Calais, was sent on 3 November 1919 and signed E.R.T.D. *"I am back at the old Dêpot again where I remain until my Kit turns up; at present it is on its way out of France. I visited G's hospital the other evening and took Margaret Deane out to dinner. I am glad you like the Imperial. I wonder when I shall be in Blighty again, a fortnight perhaps! Anyhow I am longing to be back to the Battle of the Swamps."*

Joe, who was still serving in Germany 18 months after the end of the war, wrote to Mrs Ford, 44 Sidney Road, Eastbourne, Sussex, England – sent on 7 July 1920. *"My dear Ethel, Just a P.C. to let you know I'm still alive. Will try and write a letter one day when I have time, but I seem to get very little somehow. Hope you are all getting along alright. It's lovely all round Berlin I'm sure you'd enjoy it here. It's very hot just at present but nice in the evening. How's the flat progressing? Uncle ought to hear me trying to talk German. Hope Aunt's hand is better. Love to all Joe."*

Demobilisation signalled the end of McGill's offering of wartime cards. He returned to portraying the latest fashions in both evening and swim wear and many cards featuring happy times at the seaside. Drunks and hen-pecked husbands still made an appearance but the humour was gentle and not controversial as it was in the 1950's. However, the shadow of the First World War is still to be found blighting the battlefields of France and Belgium. Between 1914 and 1918, the opposing armies fired an estimated 1.45 billion shells at each other, of which 66 million contained mustard gas or other toxic chemicals such as phosphogene or white phosphorus. Attacks were often preceded by days of non-stop bombardment of enemy positions, causing the ground to become so churned up and soft that up to a third of the shells simply failed to explode on impact. Farmers cultivating the battlefield sites now have heavier and more sophisticated tractors that plough much deeper than the lighter, earlier models. As a result, large quantities of munitions are returned to the surface – 274 tonnes in 2011. Accidents occur and lives are lost. Names are still being added to the list of casualties of war, *"mutilée dans la guerre!"*[48]

Plate 136. © 2013 Barbara Bruce Bairnsfather.
All rights reserved.

This continuing slaughter is featured on a Bruce Bainsfather card in his 8th series of "Fragments from France".

"Will you be -------- Mine!"
A PROPOSAL IN FLANDERS – plate 136 – The point of Jean's pitchfork awakens a sense of duty in a mine that shirked.

The card was sent by Mr Phillips to his daughter Vera at 29 Berkeley Street, Princes Park, Liverpool, on 31 December 1918, just seven weeks after the cessation of hostilities. *"At 2 Christian Road, Preston, Lancs. How well I can picture your smile when you look at picture on other side and so I think will 'Mother'. I have got a series and they are all very good. May send you another or two later. My fond love to <u>both of you</u> and may the New Year bring you all the good fortune & happiness it is possible to have. Ever yours affectionately, Pater. 31.12.18."* Questions that come to mind include – was Mr Phillips in the Armed Forces? If not, why was he away from home over the New Year?

In 1939, war was declared and McGill found himself once more drawing wartime cards, which featured life on the Home Front. Far fewer World War II cards were produced and some of those were very similar to those produced in the First World War. On one drawn in 1939 and nearly identical to that produced in 1916, a small boy still found time to study a map of Europe and declare, *"That's where Dad is!"*

24. OTHER TYPES OF CARDS USED DURING THE WAR

A

NO NEWS – ONLY THE SAME THING OVER AND OVER AGAIN! (Also in French) – Inter-Art Co. card – "NEW LOVE" series (No 252) – drawn by Fred Spurgin. Posted via the censor on 8 August 1915 to Miss Thomson, V.A.D. Hospital, 2 Church Road, Ashford, Kent, England. *"Dearest, It is just a card saying Goodbye. Love Frank. Am writing shortly."*

A

B

B

I FEEL BOTH GLAD AND SAD TODAY –
EXCUSE ME, WHILE I SHED A TEAR
I'M GLAD YOU HAVN'T SHIRKED THE FRAY –
AND YET I'M SAD WE'RE PARTING, DEAR.

Sent by Rachel from Manchester on 3 July 1916 to Miss Nancy Woolley, Glebe Farm, Church, Stoke.

C

HAPPY CHRISTMAS – Silk French and British flags. *"To my dear sister with Xmas Greetings from your loving brother Jack."* The card is not postmarked and was most probably sent in an envelope so that it was protected. These cards were expensive, costing up to three days pay of an average soldier, which was approximately 3 shillings. They were part of a cottage industry, which saw mainly women engaged in intricate designs being hand-embroidered onto strips of silk mesh. These strips were then sent to factories for cutting and mounting as postcards and greetings cards. It is estimated that about ten million were produced.

C

CHEER UP, THE FIRST SEVEN YEARS WILL BE THE WORST

D

D

CHEER UP, THE FIRST SEVEN YEARS WILL BE THE WORST – Sent from Rathgar, Dublin (Ireland) on 27 January 1919 to Miss G Ledger, c/o Lieut. Col. Haynes, Bentley, Hants, England. *"Dear Gert, Thanks for your letter, Meme shall send what you want Gramny's arm is a great deal better I am better and back at school again why did you not bring some of the Airoplane you saw smashed home With love from Geoffrey."*

E

The 3rd Welch leaving Cardiff Castle. WELSH TROOPS PICTURE POST-CARD DAY in Aid of THE NATIONAL FUND FOR WELSH TROOPS. President, COUNTESS OF PLYMOUTH. Chairman, Mrs LLOYD GEORGE. Treasurer Sir E. VINCENT Evans. Secretary, Mr. WILLIAM LEWIS, 11 Downing Street. (Lloyd George was Chancellor of the Exchequer at the time.)

E

Convoi anglais traversant une rivière
sur un pont de bateaux

An English convey crossing a river
by means of a bridge of boats

F

F

An English convey crossing a river by means of a bridge of boats. This is a French card (Carte Postale) with a caption in French and also in English (notice the incorrect spelling of 'convoy') sent on 12 December 1914. The message and address are both written in French.

G

96   THE KING AT THE FRONT.   A greeting from the troops   "Daily Mail" Official Photograph Crown Copyright reserved

G

THE KING AT THE FRONT. A greeting from the troops. Daily Mail WAR PICTURES, Series XII (No 96). In 1916, the Press Bureau gave the Daily Mail the sole right to reproduce on postcards the pictures of the Western Front battles, taken by their official photographers – on condition that half the profits from the sale of the cards were given to Army relief funds. 200 postcards were produced and albums could be purchased for their collection.[49]

H

Camp Anglais – L'Etuve – G.B. This is a photograph of a steam room or – more likely – a steriliser. Could it be a steriliser for louse-infested uniforms?

Camp Anglais – L'Etuve - G.B.

H

The card was sent on 5 May 1918 via the censor to Miss H Joiner, 16 Gerrard St, Brighton, Sussex, England by Arthur. *"This is the camp we are at. Dear Hilda – Just a Card to let you know I am just getting over the Parting from Home now Will write again soon give my love to All. From Arthur."*

Belgian and French cards showing rural and urban scenes were frequently used by the troops. The names of the towns and villages were usually erased by the censor. The two cards showing rural scenes depict the main street in a village and children in a primary school.

I

J

K & L

One of the two urban cards, showing a tram and a harbour scene, was sent on 4 September 1916, most probably from France. The other, sent from Courtrai in Belgium, does not have the name of the town erased, as it was sent 0n 14 December1918, after the cessation of hostilities. The sender of the second card hopes to be home early 'next year' (1919).

K

L

M & N

Both at home and in the rear areas of battle zones, photographers did a roaring trade in providing soldiers with photographic images of themselves. 'M' shows a young man, the photograph taken by A E Lupton, 141 Nightingale Road, (Town indistinct) while the soldier was still in the U.K.. The card is postally unused but the back states 'POST CARD – British Made'. 'N' is a full length portrait of a soldier, with equipment slung across his chest and was almost certainly taken in France. The card is again postally unused and the back states 'CARTE POSTALE'.

M

 *N*

O, P, Q & R
Sentimental cards were available both in the U.K. and at the Front.

O
JUST BEFORE THE BATTLE, MOTHER.

Farewell, Mother, you may never, you may never, Mother,
Press me to your heart again;
But oh, you'll not forget me, Mother, you will not forget me,
If I'm numbered with the slain.

(A Bamford card.) The card was not postally used.

 *O*

P

Fondest Thoughts

I think of you, my darling,
With loving thoughts so true.
And though we apart to-day,
I think of none but you.

Although the card was not postally used, Jessie composed her own poem:
Tis hard to part with those you love
Tis hard to part that's true
But it is not so hard to part with some
As it is to part with you.
To The One I Love
From Jessie XXX

(She has also drawn a heart.)

Q

French sentiment is well represented. A card posted via the censor on 13 December 1915 to Miss Ada Spearing, Paradise Mills, Near Langport, Somerset, England, has the message *"Dear Ada, Just a card wishing you a happy Xmas and a prosperous New Year, hoping all is well as it leaves me the same at present from Uncle Fred."*
(A. Noyer, Rueil, Paris – Fabrication Française.)

R

HONNEUR – GLOIRE
Reviens couronn de laurier
L'amour t'attend au cher foyer

('*A crown of laurels and love wait for you at your dear home.*')

Card sent via the censor on 15 September 1918 to Mrs F – , c/o Mrs Pitman, 2 Mordaunt Road, The Avenue, Southampton.

"My darling Beaty, So sorry I am unable to write a letter today but will do so for certain tomorrow. Today will be the last time I shall see Fred as he leaves here in the morning. All my love, your loving husband Fred XXXXX"

S

T

S

CAIRO. – GENERAL VIEW OF BEDRECHEN VILLAGE NEAR CAIRO. Sent via the censor on 2 August 1918 to Master J Lugmore, "Brookville", New Barnet, England. *"My dear Tom, Only two (cards) this time, the last of the packet. As for more, I am away from shops but the P.O. will do many things. Your summer holiday will be just – – "* (continued on a second card, not in our possession.)

T

AT THE PROPHET BIRTHDAY – SUDAN TIMES sent via the censor on 28 December 1915 to Sergt. J Goodge, B Coy 9th Bat Lincolns Regt., Whittington Heath, Lichfield, England. *"Dear Joe, Just these few lines to you hoping to find you quite well as it me A1 up to the time of writing this. How are you all going down there. Have you got shifted yet. Have you been to Tamworth lately. Remember me to Lizzie the next time you go down. We havent been in the firing line yet but I hear that the last draft has left – – – - from Nobby"*

25. EXAMPLES OF CENSOR MARKS

Small red circular handstamp,
example 1 November 1914

Square example, 14 August 1915,
card Port Said, Egypt

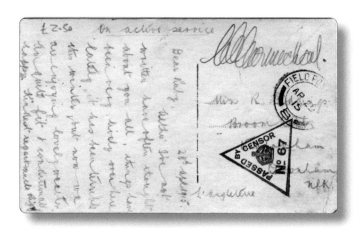

Triangular example, 29 April 1915

Hexagonal example, 4 September 1916

Oval example, 22 September 1917

Rectangular handstamp example,
17 November 1917

Rectangular handstamp example,
17 April 1918

Rectangular handstamp example,
23 October 1917

Octagonal handstamp example,
23 October 1918
Card Roma – interno, Basilica s. Pietro

Shield handstamp example,
17 December 1918
Card Buon Natale

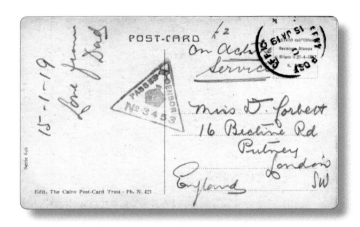

Sent 15 January 1919
Card The Cairo Postcard Trust
'CAIRO – Procession of the Holy Carpets'

McGill 'Comique' Series No 1478
Sent 19 December 1916 and
15 April 1917

REFERENCES

1. Lund, Brian – (October 2010) – *Picture Postcard Monthly* (PPM): 31.

2. Buckland, Elfreda – (1984) – *The World of Donald McGill*: 88 – 89.

3. Time Books – (1999) – *A Century in Photography – a Portrait of Britain 1900-1999*: 43.

4. van Emden R & Humphries S – (2003) – *All Quiet on the Home Front*: 9.

5. Moynahan, Brian – (1997) – *The British Century*: 94.

6. Lawer, Di – (November 2008) *Picture Postcard Monthly*: 30.

7. The Open University – (2007) – Europe in 1914 – article 312, 'Total War and Social Change: Europe 1914–1955': 50.

8. Arthur, Max – (2005) – *Last Post*: 43-44.

9. Wilton, John – (1991) – *Eastbourne Volume 2 – A Second Portrait in Old Picture Postcards*: 13-14.

10. Carden-Coyne, Dr Anna, quoted in "The Times", 26 December 2012.

11. *All Quiet on the Home Front*, op. cit.: 251-252.

12. *All Quiet on the Home Front*, op. cit.:203.

13. *All Quiet on the Home Front*, op. cit.: 213-214.

14. *All Quiet on the Home Front*t, op. cit.: 234-235.

15. Times Books – *A Century in Photographs – a Portrait of Britain 1900–1919*: 45.

16. *All Quiet on the Home Front*, op. cit.: 237.

17. *All Quiet on the Home Front*, op. cit.: 21.

18. *All Quiet on the Home Front*, op. cit.: 269.

19. Duffy, Michael – *Encyclopedia*, 22 August 2009.

20. *Last Post*, op. cit.: 47.

21. *Last Post*, op. cit.: 122.

22. Lund, Brian – *Picture Postcard Monthly* (PPM), November 2006: 41.

23. *All Quiet on the Home Front*, op. cit.:25-26.

24. Doyle, Peter – (2010) – *British Postcards of the First World War*: 32-33.

25. Brophy J & Partridge E – 2008 – *The Daily Telegraph Dictionary of Tommies' Songs and Slang*, 1914–1918: 59.

26. *All Quiet on the Home Front*, op. cit.:16.

27. *All Quiet on the Home Front*, op. cit: 189.

28. *All Quiet on the Home Front*, op. cit: 196.

29. *All Quiet on the Home Front*, op. cit: 219.

30. *All Quiet on the Home Front*, op. cit.: 254.

31. *All Quiet on the Home Front*, op. cit.: 279.

32. *All Quiet on the Home Front*, op. cit.: 254 – 255.

33. *All Quiet on the Home Front*, op. cit.: 271.

34. *All Quiet on the Home Front*, op. cit.: 150-153.

35. *All Quiet on the Home Front*, op. cit.: 160.

36. *All Quiet on the Home Front*, op. cit.: 165.

37. *All Quiet on the Home Front*, op. cit.: 171 – 172.

38. *All Quiet on the Home Front*, op. cit.: 173.

39. *All Quiet on the Home Front*, op. cit.: 57.

40. *All Quiet on the Home Front*, op. cit.: 68.

41. Hart, Peter – (2013) – *The Great War*: 393.

42. Brooks Andrew – *Picture Postcard Monthly*, April 2011: 36—38. Also the Naval & Military Press, *Soldiers Died in the Great War*, CD Rom.

43. Arthur Max – (2005) – Last Post: 45.

44. Doyle, Peter – (2010) – *British Postcards of the First World War*: 52.

45. Lawer, Diana – *Picture Postcard Monthly, Are We Downhearted? – No!* November 2010: 31-33.

46. *All Quiet on the Home Front*, op. cit.: 17.

47. *All Quiet on the Home Front*, op. cit.: 300.

48. Fletcher, Martin – *Deadly Harvest*, Telegraph Magazine, 13 July 2013: 41.

49. Monahan, Valerie – *Collecting Postcards in Colour,* 1914 – 1930, 1980: 21.

LIST OF PLATES

F = Caption also written in French
C = Passed by the Censor
n.p.u. = Not postally used

PLATE	PUBLISHER	SERIES	NUMBER	DATE USED	F	C
1	Joseph Asher & Co.		A843	July 1913		
2	Joseph Asher & Co.		1328	May 1914		
3	Joseph Asher & Co.		A1162	September 1920		
4	Joseph Asher & Co.		A466	February 1913		
5	Joseph Asher & Co.		1343	July 1914		
6	Joseph Asher & Co.		1341	April 1914		
7	Joseph Asher & Co.		1342	April 1914		
8	Gale & Polden Ltd., London, Aldershot, Portsmouth & Chatham			August 1913		
9	Inter-Art Co.	Comique	2433	August 1920	F	
10	Inter-Art Co.	Patriotic VII	864	n.p.u.		
11	Inter-Art Co.	Comique	1543	Not dated or postmarked		
12	Inter-Art Co.	Comique	1461	Not dated & no postmark visible		
13	Inter-Art Co.	Patriotic IV	811	November 1914		
14	Inter-Art Co.	R.C. illegible	959	Date on postmark		
15	Inter-Art Co.	Patriotic IV	813	October 1914		
16	Inter-Art Co.	Patriotic IV	818	November 1914		
17	Inter-Art Co.	Armee	910	Not dated & no postmark		
18	Inter-Art Co.	Armee	912	October 1915	F	C
19	Inter-Art Co.	Armee	908	March 1915		
20	Inter-Art Co.	Recruits	920	August 1915		
21	Inter-Art Co.	Recruits	921	February 1915		

PLATE	PUBLISHER	SERIES	NUMBER	DATE USED	F	C
22	Inter-Art Co.	Recruits	922	1915		
23	Inter-Art Co.	Recruits	925	April 1916		
24	Inter-Art Co.	TWO-SIX-THREE	266	August 1915		
25	Inter-Art Co.	ONE-SIX-ONE	169	December 1915		
26	Inter-Art Co.	ONE-SIX-ONE	164	n.p.u.	F	
27	Inter-Art Co.	Comique	1786	n.p.u.		
28	Inter-Art Co.	Comique	1777	March 1917		
29	Inter-Art Co.	Comique	1783	n.p.u.		
30	Inter-Art Co.	Recruits	923	February 1915		
31	Inter-Art Co.	Comique	2286	n.p.u.		
32	Inter-Art Co.	K.A.	174	n.p.u.		
33	Inter-Art Co.	Comique	1331	n.p.u.		
34	Inter-Art Co.	Comique	2054	July 1918		
35	Inter-Art Co.	Comique	2184	August 1918		
36	Inter-Art Co.	Comique	1987	Postmark illegible	F	
37	Cromptons, Eastbourne	—	—	October 1915		
38	Cromptons, Eastbourne	—	—	October 1915		
39	Inter-Art Co.	TWELVE-THIRTY-EIGHT	1243	May 1917		
40	Inter-Art Co.	THE FRONT	1217	Date not visible		
41	Inter-Art Co.	ELEVEN-TWENTY-TWO	1124	July 1916		
42	Inter-Art Co.	Comique	2049	November 1917		
43	Inter-Art Co.	Comique	2186	July 1920		
44	Inter-Art Co.	Comique	2545	November 1918	F	C
45	Inter-Art Co.	ARTISTIQUE	1431	February 1917		
46	Inter-Art Co.	ARTISTIQUE	1428	August 1917		
47	Inter-Art Co.	Comique	1474	October 1917		
48	Inter-Art Co.	TWO-O-THREE	205	Date not visible	F	
49	Inter-Art Co.	S.P.C. I	955	August 1915		
50	Inter-Art Co.	S.P.C. II	113	April 1915		
51	Inter-Art Co.	S.P.C. II	114	November 1917		
52	Inter-Art Co.	S.P.C. II	115	April 1915		

PLATE	PUBLISHER	SERIES	NUMBER	DATE USED	F	C
53	Inter-Art Co.	S.P.C. II	116	n.p.u.		
54	Inter-Art Co.	Comique	2643	n.p.u.		
55	Inter-Art Co.	PROTECTION	1042	n.p.u.		
56	Inter-Art Co.	Comique	1727	Not dated or postmarked		
57	Inter-Art Co.	Comique	2131	Not dated or postmarked		
58	Inter-Art Co.	Comique	2391	Date not visible		
59	Inter-Art Co.	Comique	2052	n.p.u.		
60	Inter-Art Co.	Comique	2791	August 1919		
61	Inter-Art Co.	Comique	1460	August 1916		
62	Inter-Art Co.	Comique	1395	October 1917	F	
63	Inter-Art Co.	TWELVE-THIRTY-EIGHT	1238	April 1916		
64	Inter-Art Co.	Comique	1386	July 1916	F	
65	Inter-Art Co.	Comique	1332	July 1916		
66	Inter-Art Co.	Comique	1882	July 1917		
67	Inter-Art Co.	Comique	2331	n.p.u.		
68	Bystander's Fragments from France		Series 1	n.p.u.		
69	Bystander's Fragments from France		Series 2	n.p.u.		
70	Bystander's Fragments from France		Series 2	January 1917		
71	Inter-Art Co.	Comique	2149	1917		
72	Inter-Art Co.	Comique	1709	April 1917		
73	Inter-Art Co.	Comique	1610	n.p.u.	F	
74	Inter-Art Co.	THE FRONT	1223	Not dated or postmarked	F	
75	Inter-Art Co.	Comique	2396	August 1918		
76	Inter-Art Co.	Comique	2390	May 1918		
77	Inter-Art Co.	Comique	2445	September 1918		
78	Inter-Art Co.	Comique	2393	August 1918		

PLATE	PUBLISHER	SERIES	NUMBER	DATE USED	F	C
79	Inter-Art Co.	Comique	2430	December 1918		
80	Inter-Art Co.	Comique	2431	October 1919		
81						
	Inter-Art Co.	Comique	2386	January 1919		
82	Inter-Art Co.	Comique	2389	Not dated or postmarked		
83	Inter-Art Co.	TWO-EIGHT-ONE	282	August 1915		
84	Inter-Art Co.	Comique	1784	August 1917		
85	Inter-Art Co.	Comique	2190	n.p.u.		
86	Inter-Art Co.	Comique	2412	September 1918		
87	Inter-Art Co.	Comique	1546	Not dated or postmarked		
88	Inter-Art Co.	Comique	1475	Postmark illegible		
89	Inter-Art Co.	TWO-EIGHT-ONE	281	October 1915		
90	Inter-Art Co.	PROTECTION	1038	August 1915		
91	Inter-Art Co.	Comique	2194	n.p.u.		
92	Inter-Art Co.	TWO-EIGHT-ONE	290	August 1916		
93	Inter-Art Co.	TWO-SIX-THREE	265	April 1916		
94	Inter-Art Co.	Comique	1991	August 1918		
95	Inter-Art Co.	FIRST LINE	1347	Not dated or postmarked	F	
96	Inter-Art Co.	FIRST LINE	1354	August 1916?		
97	Inter-Art Co.	Comique	2008	June 1918		
98	Inter-Art Co.	Comique	2007	April 1918		
99	Inter-Art Co.	Comique	1470	September 1918	F	
100	Inter-Art Co.	Comique	2011	September 1918	F	
101	Inter-Art Co.	TWELVE-SIXTY-EIGHT	1269	October 1917	F	C
102	Inter-Art Co.	Comique	2010	February 1918		
103	Inter-Art Co.	Series not stated	935	n.p.u.		
104	Inter-Art Co.	TWO-EIGHT-ONE	287	n.p.u.		
105	Inter-Art Co.	Comique	1996	December 1918		
106	Inter-Art Co.	TWELVE-SIX-EIGHT	1271	Not dated or postmarked		

PLATE	PUBLISHER	SERIES	NUMBER	DATE USED	F	C
107	Inter-Art Co.	Comique	1700	June 1917		
108	Envelope	Passed by censor		December 1914		
109	Inter-Art Co.	ONE-SIX-ONE	165	n.p.u.		
110	Inter-Art Co.	Comique	2673	April 1919		
111	FIELD SERVICE POST CARD	(Address side)		July 1917		
112	FIELD SERVICE POST CARD	(Message side)		July 1917		
113	Inter-Art Co.	Comique	1466	November 1916	F	
114	Inter-Art Co.	Comique	1716	May 1917	F	C
115	Inter-Art Co.	Comique	1486	Not dated or postmarked	F	
116	Inter-Art Co.	Comique	1787	n.p.u.		
117	Inter-Art Co.	Comique	1465	September 1917	F	C
118	Inter-Art Co.	Comique	2566	Not dated or postmarked		
119	Inter-Art Co.	Comique	1618	January 1918	F	C
120	Inter-Art Co.	Comique	1986	Not dated or postmarked	F	
121	Inter-Art Co.	Comique	2128	n.p.u.		
122	Inter-Art Co.	I 2 U	1045	August 1915		
123	Inter-Art Co.	Comique	2275	August 1918		
124	Inter-Art Co.	Patriotic IV	817	Not dated or postmarked		
125	Inter-Art Co.	TWELVE-SEVEN-FOUR	1278	Date not legible		
126	Inter-Art Co.	Comique	1661	May 1917		
127	Inter-Art Co.	Comique	2002	November 1917		
128	Inter-Art Co.	Comique	2281	n.p.u.		
129	Inter-Art Co.	Comique	2328	? 1919		
130	A.H. Fry, Brighton	Official photograph issued by the Corporation of Brighton with the assistance of the military authorities	4 The Dome	June 1915		

PLATE	PUBLISHER	SERIES	NUMBER	DATE USED	F	C
131	A.H. Fry, Brighton	Official photograph issued by the Corporation of Brighton with the assistance of the military authorities	9 Royal Pavilion, Ward 5 Music Room	n.p.u.		
132	Inter-Art Co.	Comique	1806	May 1917		
133	Inter-Art Co.	Comique	2642	May 1919		
134	Inter-Art Co.	Comique	1652	January 1919		
135	Inter-Art Co.	Comique	1662	March 1919		
136	Bystander's Fragments from France		Series 8	December 1918		

GLOSSARY

ANZAC – Australian and New Zealand Army Corps

AOE – (Error by sender?) Probably meant AOC (Army Ordnance Corps) or AOD (Army Ordnance Depot)

APO – Army Post Office

ASC – Army Service Corps

BAT/BN – Battalion

BEF – British Expeditionary Force

BULLING – Bull polishing, spit polishing or spit shining to leave one's boots as shiny as a mirror for inspection.

COL – Colonel

COY – Company

DRAFT – Conscription. Began when the British government passed the Military Service Act in 1916. The act specified that single men aged 18 to 41 years old were liable to be called up for military service.

GHQ – General Head Quarters

GN/GNR – Gunner

HEATH ROBINSON – British cartoonist and illustrator best known for designing fantastically complicated machines. Phrase used to describe absurdly complex, makeshift contraptions.

HMS – His Majesty's Ship

IN BLUES – When soldiers were sent back to the UK for hospitalisation they were issued with hospital uniform consisting of a blue single-breasted jacket and blue trousers, a white shirt and a red tie. Also known as the 'blue invalid uniform', 'hospital suit' and 'hospital blues'.

IN THE PINK – In perfect condition, especially of health.

LANCE CORP – Lance Corporal

LIEUT – Lieutenant

MO – Medical Officer

NCO – Non-commissioned Officer

OAS – On Active Service

OTC – The Officers' Training Corps (OTC) is a part of the British Territorial Army (now Army Reserve) which provides military leadership training to students at British universities. During the Great War some 30,000 officers passed through.

PTE – Private

RAMC – Royal Army Medical Corps

REVEILLE – A bugle call, trumpet or pipes call chiefly used to wake personnel at sunrise. The name comes from the French word for 'wake up'.

SAPR – Sapper

THE COLOURS – A regiment's colours, or flags, were used as rallying points in battle hence 'rally to the colours' or 'rally round the flag'.

TOP HOLE – Excellent

U-BOATS – German word for submarine

VAD – Voluntary Aid Detachment. Provided field nursing services, mainly in hospitals, in the United Kingdom and various other countries in the British Empire and played a crucial role during the Great War.

YMCA – Young Man's Christian Association. Along with other (particularly religious) organisations, the YMCA established recreation centres throughout the United Kingdom, providing a cup of tea, sandwiches or other refreshments, and reading materials. Many of these centres were at or near railway stations or other places where large numbers of troops would be passing. By the end of 1915, this service had spread to provide hundreds of road side canteens on the battlefields of France and Flanders.

ND - #0178 - 270225 - C132 - 270/210/9 - PB - 9781908487988 - Gloss Lamination